FOOTBALL 50

Joy Bhattacharjya is a cricket analyst and is currently hosting the Cricbuzz IPL Live 2026. He runs a professional volleyball league and was the project director for the FIFA U-17 World Cup, the team director for the Kolkata Knight Riders (including two championship seasons), head of programming for History channel and National Geographic channel for South Asia and head of production for ESPN Star Sports. He also designed India's first ever fantasy sports game, Super Selector, for ESPN Star Sports. Joy is a columnist, active quizzer, sports presenter and analyst and currently resides in Delhi.

Aniket Mishra hailing from Delhi is a disciplined runner, avid quizzer and a football enthusiast. He works with FIFA and has been associated with over five editions of the World Cup (a mix of the men's and women's editions). He is the author of *Know Thy Dhoni* (2020), *The IPL Quiz Book* (2021), *125 Years of the Olympics* (2024) and more. These books are a testament of his passion and showcase his flair for writing. He has an MPhil in Comparative Literature from Delhi University and is also the founder of Barefoot Sports Quizzing Festival (2012) that has seen 14 editions.

Aniket Mishra (left) with Joy Bhattacharjya (right) at the 2001 ESPN School quiz. They have collaborated on many projects in their 25-year-long association.

THE ULTIMATE
COMPANION TO 9 DECADES
OF THE WORLD CUP

FOOTBALL 500

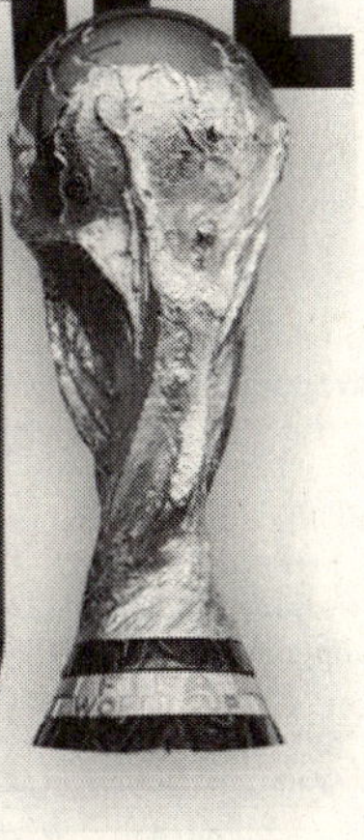

JOY BHATTACHARJYA
ANIKET MISHRA

hachette
INDIA

First published in paperback in 2026 by Hachette India
(Registered name: Hachette Book Publishing India Pvt. Ltd)
An Hachette UK company
www.hachetteindia.com

1

The copyright details and credits for the photographs in the book begin on page 246.

ISBN 978-93-5731-578-4

Hachette Book Publishing India Pvt. Ltd
4th & 5th Floors, Corporate Centre
Plot No. 94, Sector 44, Gurugram – 122003, India

Typeset by Manmohan Kumar, Delhi

Printed and bound in India
by Manipal Technologies Limited

FSC
www.fsc.org
MIX
Paper | Supporting responsible forestry
FSC™ C043100

CONTENTS

Foreword *ix*
Authors' Notes *xi*

1930, Uruguay 1
1934, Italy 12
1938, France 23
1950, Brazil 33
1954, Switzerland 45
1958, Sweden 56
1962, Chile 67
1966, England 78
1970, Mexico 88
1974, West Germany 97
1978, Argentina 107
Images, 1930–78 117
1982, Spain 131
1986, Mexico 141
1990, Italy 150
1994, USA 159
1998, France 169
2002, Korea–Japan 178
2006, Germany 187
2010, South Africa 196
2014, Brazil 205
2018, Russia 213
2022, Qatar 222
Images, 1982–2022 231

Image Copyright Information *246*

10
10

FOREWORD

There are tournaments, and then there is the World Cup.

Once every four years, the world seems to share one pulse and decides to speak a unified language – of the love for a single sport. Flags emerge from windows. Sleep becomes negotiable. Strangers lean into conversations with a familiarity normally reserved for old friends. Somewhere a radio crackles, somewhere a bar erupts, somewhere a child sees a goal and quietly decides what the rest of their life might look like.

This book is about that tournament. But it is also about us.

The World Cup is not merely a competition between nations; it is a mirror held up to the world. Inside it you will find artistry and anxiety, courage and collapse, genius and occasionally glorious absurdity. Football, after all, is a simple game that insists on complex emotions.

The beauty of the event lies partly in its unpredictability. A nation may arrive with history on its shoulders and leave with its pride bruised. Another may arrive unnoticed and suddenly discover that belief is a muscle it never knew it possessed. The tournament has always had room for both the expected and the miraculous. In many ways the World Cup is football's most democratic theatre. For a few weeks, pedigree counts for less than courage. Reputation dissolves under the glare of floodlights. The ball rolls, the whistle blows and history becomes negotiable.

This book travels through that history.

It moves from the early years when the tournament felt like a daring experiment to the modern era when it has become one of the planet's most watched spectacles. It carries us through political tensions and cultural shifts, through tactical revolutions and moments of pure instinct. Along the way we see how football has grown, not merely in scale, but in meaning.

So as you turn these pages, think of this not merely as a chronicle of records and trivia from tournaments won and lost. Think of it as a collection of human stories stitched together by the shared love for a sport.

Some of them will make you think.

Some may make you smile.

A few might even make you believe in impossible things again.

And if that happens, then you will understand what the World Cup has always been: not just sport's greatest competition, but its most compelling story.

– Bhaichung Bhutia
Former captain Indian football team

AUTHORS' NOTES

My first distinct World Cup memory was watching Dirceu of Brazil score from what seemed to be an impossibly long distance against Italy in the 3rd place play offs in 1978. And, on the scant evidence of a grainy image on a black and white EC television set, I had adopted a football team for life.

I used to have a party trick which almost never let me down. When I met someone for the first time, based on their age, I'd hazard a guess on which football team they supported.

It wasn't difficult at all. So many of my friends who had seen the fabled and star-crossed Brazilian team of 1982 play magical football stayed with Brazil. And those a little younger, whose first glimpse of the World Cup was staying up late into the night watching Maradona run rampant in Mexico '86, usually supported the blue and white of Argentina for life. And if they started watching football after Maradona called it a day, it was usually Brazil once again.

Football World Cups are as close to a global party as you can get. And I feel sometimes it's even better if you get there without your national team in attendance. For then, you can avidly follow your favourite, your second favourite and even enjoy a first time crush – the Danes in 1986, Roger Milla and Cameroon in 1990 or Senegal in 2002. And every tournament is an emotional roller coaster as your chosen teams excel or ingloriously crash out.

If T.S. Eliot famously measured his life in coffee spoons, I usually recount my days with the year Sócrates and Zico toyed with the opposition midfield or the year Baggio shot into the void or the year when Iniesta finally redeemed the Spanish.

And who is to say that isn't a better way.

– Joy Bhattacharjya

***

Time is measured differently when the football World Cup arrives. We do not age in years, but in tournaments. My first sporting memory is hearing of a Brazilian striker not showing up at his best in a World Cup final – that was Ronaldo in 1998; four years later, I was old enough to be excited for his redemption at the Yokohama stadium. As years passed, I vicariously experienced Diego Maradona dancing through the English defence, turning a football pitch into his private canvas and related heartbreak to Roberto Baggio standing with his hands on his hips, staring into the abyss of a Californian afternoon, his penalty sailing into the blue.

Every four years, the earth seemingly pauses its rotation, holding its breath for around a month of exquisite agony and unfiltered joy.

This is not merely a sporting event; it is a global communion. A time when humanity agrees to speak a single, uncorrupted language.

Out there, on that perfectly manicured geometry of green, men become a myth. They carry the hopes of entire nations on their shoulders – a fragile, terrifying burden that can crush the ordinary and elevate the genius to immortality. Football at this level is stripped of its domestic mundane. It becomes an enterprising, breathless ballet. It can be found in the sudden, predatory swerve of Kylian Mbappé; the quiet, surgical geometry of Lionel Messi plotting a pass before the world has even seen the angle or Cristiano Ronaldo bending a free kick with surgical precision over a wall of defenders in the dying minutes of a game; the sheer, elemental force of a roaring stadium pressing down on a lone goalkeeper can only be experienced vicariously.

We watch because we are drawn to this vulnerability. We watch to see grown men weep into the turf, their boyhood dreams dissolving beneath the glare of stadium lights. We watch because, in those ninety minutes, our complex world is distilled into a perfect, simple drama. There is a purity to the World Cup that defies the cynic. It is a theatre where the deepest human emotions are displayed and each emotion depicted as the boldest colours ever painted.

To write about the World Cup is to write about heroes and gods. It is to trace the lineage of Pelé's joyous leaps, Zidane's brooding artistry and the countless, nameless defenders who sacrificed their chance at glory and fame, their youth and bodies, almost like ghosts, for a flag. It is to understand that a single touch of the ball can alter the mood of a continent.

This book is a chronicle of those touches. It is a journey through the archives of our collective memory and the blinding glare of a gold trophy lifted into the confetti-filled sky. It is about the romance of *the beautiful game* when the stakes are absolute.

Hope it helps you relive the magic. Happy reading.

– Aniket Mishra

1930, URUGUAY

STORIES

Ship of Dreams

In June 1930, SS *Conte Verde*, an elegant Italian transatlantic liner built in Scotland for the Genoese Lloyd Sabaudo line, famously became the vessel that carried several national football teams, referees, officials and even the World Cup trophy itself across the Atlantic, placing it at the centre of the first World Cup's history.

It set sail from Genoa with the Romanian national football team aboard, and over the next days, made stops at Villefranche-sur-Mer on the French Riviera, where the France national football team boarded along with the then president of FIFA, Jules Rimet, three European referees, and the World Cup trophy itself packed in Rimet's suitcase. It then stopped over in Barcelona where it picked up the Belgium national football team. After leaving Europe, it navigated the Atlantic and, just over a week later, reached Rio de Janeiro, where the Brazilian team came aboard.

On 4 July 1930, after over a fortnight, it docked in Montevideo, in time for the start of the tournament.

Aboard the *Conte Verde*, the journey was more than mere travel. For many players, the ship became a temporary training ground and communal living space. According to accounts, footballers ran on deck, stretched, jumped stairs, lifted weights and even swam when weather permitted.

An arrangement such as this was a bold logistical solution, and proved essential in enabling European teams to be represented in Montevideo. At a time when economic depression and travel costs discouraged many teams, the *Conte Verde*'s voyage made participation possible.

In many ways, the journey aboard the *Conte Verde* symbolizes more than just geographic transit – it represented the ambition to bring together nations for a common sporting purpose long before the age of mass air travel. The 1930 World Cup might not have been global in its truest sense without this Italian carrier.

A Cauldron of Champions

When Uruguay was selected to host the first FIFA World Cup in 1930, the young nation embraced the decision with pride and ambition. Having won back-to-back Olympic gold medals in football in 1924 and 1928, Uruguay saw the World Cup as a chance not only to showcase its sporting supremacy but also to commemorate a historic milestone: the centenary of the 1830 Constitution. To honour both achievements, the government and football authorities announced the construction of a new stadium of unprecedented scale, to be built in Montevideo in time for the tournament.

The plan was visionary and risky in equal measure. The chosen site in Parque Batlle provided ample space, but the timeline was daunting: construction effectively had to be completed in less than a year. Architect Juan Antonio Scasso was tasked with designing a stadium capable of seating tens of thousands of spectators while also functioning as a national monument. His vision took the form of a vast concrete bowl, open to the sky, with steeply rising stands encircling the pitch and a monumental tower visible across the city.

Work began in July 1929 and, despite harsh conditions and several obstacles, on 18 July 1930, the stadium – Estadio Centenario – was inaugurated, exactly 100 years after Uruguay adopted its first constitution. The inaugural match, Uruguay vs Peru, marked the beginning not only of World Cup history within its walls but also of the Centenario's place in the emotional landscape of the country.

By the time the final was played there, the stadium had become inseparable from the team's triumph and the nation's pride.

Estadio Centenario stood as proof that Uruguay, though small in population, was powerful in ambition and organizational capacity. The stadium was almost symbolic of the grand execution of the first ever global extravaganza. The Tower of Homage, rising above the grandstands, honoured national heroes and Olympic athletes. The stadium's scale established it as one of the great sporting venues of its era, and one that would endure long after the last whistle of 1930.

Chloroform on a Football Field

Among the many wild and half-forgotten stories from the first FIFA World Cup in 1930, few are as strange or as enduring as the tale of the American trainer who supposedly knocked himself unconscious by inhaling chloroform during a match. The incident, which has since taken on near-mythical status, offers a vivid window into the raw, chaotic and improvisational nature of early international football.

The 1930 World Cup semi-final between the United States and Argentina was already expected to be rugged, and it lived up to its billing. Midway through the first half, an American player suffered a severe facial injury after a rough challenge. At a time when substitutes were not permitted and protective medical protocols barely existed, team staff were the only lifeline for injured players. Thus the American trainer, John 'Jock' Coll, sprinted onto the pitch carrying a small wooden medical box filled with rudimentary supplies.

What happened next has become almost legendary. In countless retellings, Coll is said to have dropped his medical kit while rushing to the player. Inside was a bottle of chloroform, which shattered on the ground. As Coll leaned down to gather the pieces, he inhaled the fumes, instantly passed out and had to be carried off on a stretcher, leaving the injured American footballer unattended.

There is, however, a less dramatic historical version. An official report from the American team later indicated that Coll did not faint due to chloroform. Instead, during the chaotic treatment, with players from both sides crowding and shouting, Coll's smelling salts were knocked from his hand, striking the injured player in the eyes. The resulting confusion, shouting and stumbling by both men may have later evolved into the more theatrical 'chloroform knockout' narrative.

Whichever version is closest to reality, the story has survived because it captures the spirit of 1930 football more truthfully than scorelines ever could. The first World Cup was an event of rough-edged emotion, lacking today's medical systems, substitution rules and officiating discipline. On-field injuries were often treated with whatever chemicals, gauze or salts a trainer could carry in a box. In that environment, an accident like Coll's seems entirely believable!

Different Match Balls in Different Halves

A notable point of contention before the final of the 1930 World Cup was the choice of ball for the decisive match. With both Argentina and Uruguay insisting on using their own balls, the Belgian referee, John Langenus, brokered a compromise: each team would supply its own ball, and one would be used in the first half and the other in the second.

The result: the first half was played with Argentina's ball, the lighter, smaller 12-panel model known as the 'Tiento', while the second half was contested with Uruguay's choice, the heavier, more substantial 11-panel leather ball called the 'T-Model'.

The split-ball match turned out to be almost poetic. In the first half, with the Tiento, Argentina led 2–1 at half-time. But once the T-Model was brought in for the second half, the game turned on its head. The hosts rallied strongly and scored three goals to win 4–2, thereby becoming the first-ever World Cup champions.

This dramatic shift fuelled the legend of the final; some accounts point to the change of ball as symbolizing a shift in momentum, of 'home advantage' regained by Uruguay, embodied not just in morale but in the very physical instrument of the game.

In some ways, the two-ball story encapsulates the spirit of that inaugural World Cup: humble, handcrafted balls; a fragile, cross-continental organization; passionate rivalry; and improvisation. It stands in stark contrast to the modern era of high-tech and standardized match balls used across the globe.

The legacy of the dual-ball final remains one of the most evocative anecdotes in World Cup history. The T-Model ball used by Uruguay in the second half is preserved (or at least represented by replicas) in football museums, a tangible relic of the sport's beginnings on the global stage.

A Cramped Ferry Ride to Attend a World Cup Final

When Uruguay and Argentina met in the final, for many in Buenos Aires, it was a clash of national pride, honour and identity. Thousands of Argentine supporters felt compelled to witness the match in person. Their journey to Montevideo remains one of the most emotional and dramatic fan pilgrimages in the early history of world football.

Although Río de la Plata or La Plata River separated the two capitals only by a relatively short distance, it was the scale of support, the sheer number of fans, that was unprecedented. Any vessel capable of carrying passengers – ferries, commercial boats, river cruisers, smaller hired craft – was pressed into service. Contemporary estimates suggest that 10,000–15,000 Argentine fans crossed the river, many crammed into overcrowded boats, fuelled not by comfort but passion. They sang chants and waved flags throughout the crossing, adopting a slogan that encapsulated their mentality: '*Victoria o muerte* (Victory or death)'.

Their arrival brought scenes of congestion and chaos. Montevideo's port, unused to receiving such crowds at once, struggled to process the influx. Roads to the stadium clogged up, and for many, simply disembarking and reaching the Estadio Centenario became a challenge. Some supporters reportedly never made it inside before kick-off despite hours of effort. The stadium gates opened six hours before the match to avoid disorder. Security was tight and rival tensions high; fans were searched for weapons as they entered. Nonetheless, the terraces filled rapidly, and by early afternoon the bowl-shaped stadium was bursting with expectation.

Inside, the atmosphere was electric. The newly built Centenario was hosting its biggest moment, and the rivalry between the two nations crackled in every part of the ground. For Argentine supporters, the match's first half was a dream. Their team overturned an early Uruguayan lead and went into the break 2–1 ahead. But in the second half, Uruguay fought back with ferocious determination. Two goals turned the game around, and a late fourth sealed the outcome. The stadium erupted on one side and fell into stunned silence on the other. For the Argentines who had crossed the river, the final whistle was heartbreak in its purest form: a dream shattered, not for lack of support, but in spite of it.

The contrast between the two capitals the next day could not have been sharper. Uruguay declared a national holiday; Montevideo celebrated triumph deep into the night. Buenos Aires, by contrast, seethed with disappointment. Angry crowds reportedly gathered near the Uruguayan consulate, venting frustration that extended beyond sport.

Yet the story of those travelling fans is not defined solely by defeat. Their journey symbolized the birth of global supporter culture, long before packaged tourism, charter flights or organized fan zones. It showed how football could inspire real sacrifice, collective movement and emotional investment. In 1930, around 15,000 people crossed the river not because it was easy, but because the love of the game compelled them.

QUIZ

Questions

Kick-Off

1. Nicknamed 'El Manco', Héctor Castro scored the first goal as well as a goal in the final for the hosts and eventual winners, Uruguay. Why is his achievement considered unique?
2. Starting in 1920 in Antwerp, football's governing body, FIFA, were tasked with overseeing the Olympic Football Tournament (earlier organized by the IOC). At the time, it was deemed, like other sports, the world championship for football. For what particular reason did FIFA soon decide to be more 'inclusive' and organize a World Cup of their own?
3. Constructed in 1923, Italian passenger liner SS *Conte Verde* remains etched in the annals of World Cup history. What coveted item accompanied three teams and the then president of FIFA, Jules Rimet, during its historic 15-day transatlantic voyage to Montevideo in 1930?
4. Who was the only surviving member of the 1930 French squad to witness France win the World Cup in 1998 on home soil? Holding the distinction of scoring the first ever FIFA World Cup goal, he passed away in 2005 at the age of 97, having lived through both the inaugural tournament and the 1998 World Cup.
5. Refereeing disputes were common, but Bolivian Ulises Saucedo's officiating in the Argentina vs Mexico match, which Argentina won 6–3, was perhaps the most controversial. What other role did Saucedo have at the tournament – one that made his decision to award three penalties to Argentina seem even more 'unsportsmanlike'?

Extra-Time

6. At this edition of the World Cup, what now-common system was used to adjudicate the United States as the third-placed

team in the tournament, ahead of Yugoslavia, who too were losing semi-finalists?

7. In the United States' 3–0 victory over Paraguay, there was uncertainty over the identity of the scorer of the second goal. It took 76 years before Bert Patenaude was rightfully adjudged to be the scorer. What record is he thus now rightfully credited with, one that had belonged to Argentina's Guillermo Stábile until 2006?
8. The great Luis Monti reportedly received death threats in the lead-up to the final against Uruguay. He did not let that act as a deterrent and turned up for the game that his team eventually lost. How did this appearance contribute to a unique distinction that he has held since 1934?
9. Andrés Mazali was a true multi-sport genius. Apart from being a double Olympic gold medalist in football for Uruguay, he was the 1920 South American champion in the 400 metres hurdles and also played basketball for the famed Olimpia team. For what rather frivolous reason was he ejected from the squad for the World Cup, thus missing out on being part of a list that had seven entries in 1930 and includes Lionel Messi and Ángel Di María among its latest additions in 2022?
10. Which team's participation at the inaugural FIFA World Cup was a direct result of King Carol II's passion for football, having personally negotiated with players' employers to grant them three-month leaves of absence and guaranteed that their jobs would be secure upon their return?

Shoot-Out

11. The first ever World Cup had no qualifiers; invitations were sent to all FIFA member associations, and while many declined, the tournament was set to be hosted with 16 teams from five continents. Eventually, though, three teams from Asia and Africa couldn't make the journey to Uruguay for the tournament. If Japan and Egypt were two of those countries,

which was the third – one that has still not qualified to play in a World Cup?

12. Héctor Scarone was one of football's earliest superstars. He won the South American Championship four times and the Olympic gold medal twice before winning the 1930 World Cup. During that tournament, his goal against Romania puts him as the last – and most recent – entrant in which list, one that Bart McGhee of the United States had become the first to join earlier?
13. Around 2006, a local architect Héctor Benech, tracked down aerial photographs from 1926, overlaid them onto modern maps, and managed to pinpoint a spot long thought lost. And a small sculpture (or monument) was installed in a Montevideo neighbourhood. What stands there today, among ordinary houses and city streets – a quiet, humble reminder of a landmark moment that changed football history?
14. The famous 'Winged Victory' statue housed in the Louvre in France is the ancient Hellenistic sculpture of Nike of Samothrace. Given Nike's mythical status, what was loosely – and rather aptly – based on this iconic structure?
15. The first official logbook of international football matches was kept at 67 Nicolaas Maesstraat in Amsterdam till 1932. The carefully curated records were maintained by Cornelis August Wilhelm Hirschman, who advocated the move to hold matches between international teams and not just clubs based on these logs. What position did he hold in FIFA when the first World Cup was hosted, one that saw a historic appointment in 2016?

Anagrams

Unscramble the following to name five of the first goalscorers for their respective countries at the inaugural World Cup. If it helps, the names of their countries are mentioned next to the anagrams.

Note: Diacritics such as accents or tildes have been omitted.

1. ANNULERULETIC (France)
2. ANACONJURER (Mexico)
3. ALATEBUDDERS (Romania)
4. CHARTRESCOOT (Uruguay)
5. ABUTTERNEAPED (United States of America)

ANSWER KEY

Answers to Questions

1. He was the only amputee to score in a FIFA World Cup final. (El Manco translates to one-armed or maimed.)
2. Only amateurs were allowed to compete at the Olympic Games.
3. The FIFA World Cup trophy
4. Lucien Laurent
5. He was the coach of the Bolivian team. (This was an only instance of a team's coach also being appointed as a referee for a World Cup.)
6. Goal difference (Both Yugoslavia and Unites States scored 6 goals in the group stage, but the former had also conceded a goal and were thus relegated to fourth spot in tournament rankings.)
7. First ever FIFA World Cup hat-trick
8. He is the only player to contest two FIFA World Cup finals for two teams. (He competed for Italy at the 1934 edition.)
9. He broke a curfew to go out on a date!
10. Romania
11. Thailand (then called Siam)
12. FIFA World Cup goalscorers born in the nineteenth century
13. The exact spot where the first ever FIFA World Cup goal was scored, now marked by a small monument.
14. The Jules Rimet Trophy (originally called 'Victory')
15. Secretary General (The historic appointment was of Fatma Samoura, the first woman and the first African to hold that post.)

Solutions to Anagrams

1. Lucien Laurent
2. Juan Carreno
3. Adalbert Desu
4. Hector Castro
5. Bert Patenaude

1934, ITALY

STORIES

Politicizing the Beautiful Game

The 1934 FIFA World Cup remains one of the most politically charged editions in the history of the sport, not merely because Italy won, but because the host, Benito Mussolini, turned football into an instrument of propaganda.

In the early 1930s, Italy's position in the international sphere was complex. Mussolini wanted to project his nation as modern, disciplined and ascendant. Hosting the World Cup offered the perfect canvas. Millions across Europe would watch, and millions of Italians would be persuaded that their country was admired and respected abroad. Accordingly, the state poured resources into stadiums, infrastructure and mass mobilization. Venues were not only modernized; they were reshaped to reflect fascist aesthetics, with monumental facades and inscriptions extolling the regime, and in some cases renamed after Fascist leaders.

Also, for Mussolini, success on the pitch mattered as much as the spectacle outside it. Italy simply had to win. The national team was reinforced by foreign-born players of Italian descent, particularly from Argentina and Uruguay, an approach framed as proof of the diaspora's loyalty to the homeland. Selection became both cultural and political, with the team serving as an extension of the state rather than an independent sporting institution.

Throughout the tournament, the leader's shadow hovered over every Italian match. His personal presence in the stands was unmistakable. And allegations later emerged which suggested that referees and officials were pressured behind closed doors.

When Italy defeated Czechoslovakia in the final, the celebrations were instantly absorbed into the machinery of propaganda. Newspapers heralded the victory as a demonstration of national superiority – and parades and speeches folded the footballers into the myth of fascist strength.

The 1934 World Cup is thus remembered still not only for the sporting achievements, but for everything that happened around it.

The Tragic Genius

In the pantheon of football's early greats, few figures shine with the bittersweet brilliance of Matthias Sindelar. To read his story is to confront how beauty and tragedy sometimes coexist. The 1934 World Cup in Italy should have been a platform for Sindelar to etch his artistry into sporting immortality.

Sindelar arrived at the World Cup as the heartbeat of Austria's famous Wunderteam, a side that was deemed invincible. Their quarter-final win over Hungary set up a semi-final clash with hosts Italy. The game in Milan turned out to be much more than just football. It unfolded under the watchful eye of Mussolini and, according to legend, with refereeing that leaned decisively towards the home side. Sindelar later recalled that it felt like playing against more than eleven players, a sentiment echoed by teammates and journalists. Austria narrowly lost, and the Wunderteam left the tournament feeling they had been denied a fair chance. It was the closest Sindelar ever came to lifting world football's greatest prize.

After 1934, the world around Sindelar changed faster than football could keep up. Europe descended towards turmoil. Austria was annexed by Nazi Germany in 1938 in the Anschluss, erasing the independent nation whose footballing identity Sindelar had embodied. Nazi authorities sought to merge Austria's players into the German national team, expecting Sindelar to become a symbol of the new regime. That expectation proved to be their miscalculation.

Sindelar refused.

Accounts differ – some say Sindelar cited age and injury; others say he openly rejected the idea of representing a team created through oppression. The most famous moment came during the final friendly match between the recently annexed Austria and Nazi-controlled Germany in April 1938. Sindelar scored a goal, celebrated defiantly near dignitaries in the stands, and Austria won 2–0. To many, the act became symbolic, a moment in which one of the greatest footballers ever was asserting his freedom against cruelty.

On 23 January 1939, Matthias Sindelar and his partner were found dead in their apartment. Official reports cited carbon-monoxide poisoning, possibly accidental. But whispers of foul play have never vanished. In death, as in life, the man who was nicknamed 'Der Papierene' for his slender frame remained elusive: delicate as paper, yet impossible to bend.

A New 'Unusual' Ball

The tournament's official ball, the Federale 102, played an undeniable role in shaping how the competition unfolded.

Made in Italy specifically for the World Cup, it was built from tanned leather panels stitched by hand and sealed by a lace that enclosed the inner bladder. Its construction made it heavier than modern footballs and more unpredictable in the air. When wet, the ball absorbed water, becoming even heavier, and turned every header into an act of fearlessness and every shot into a test of technique and courage.

The nature of the ball dictated the style of play, and thus the 1934 tournament became a showcase of mastery – and sometimes a lack of it – in controlling the ball. Strikers like Angelo Schiavio and Oldřich Nejedlý became legends not only because they scored the most, but because they mastered a ball that resisted finesse. Shooting hard and low was often the smartest option, and defenders had to brace for collisions as much as anticipate passes.

Players such as Matthias Sindelar and Giuseppe Meazza proved that the ill-reputed ball could be tamed and are thus revered even today for their performances. Sindelar in particular was so good that he was nicknamed 'the Mozart of Football'.

In the decades that followed, match ball technology evolved rapidly, with synthetic materials replacing leather, the disappearance of laces and aerodynamics becoming more increasingly refined. It can no longer give a distinct advantage to any team, but in 1934, that wasn't the case.

So Close, Yet So Far

Long before Geoff Hurst's famous 'ghost goal' from the final of the 1966 World Cup, there was Jaroslav Bouček's effort in 1934.

In the final between Italy and Czechoslovakia, with the score delicately poised at 1–0 to the Czechs, a single shot struck the inside of the post and rebounded away. Minutes later, Italy equalized, forced extra time and went on to win 2–1. For Czechoslovakia, a generation of players, and a nation that would soon be consumed by war, that strike against the woodwork became a symbol of what might have been, a moment when the world title was within reach and then gone.

Czechoslovakia had stunned the world by reaching the final with tactical intelligence, discipline and the brilliance of forward Antonín Puč and goalkeeper František Plánička. For most of the final, they matched Italy stride for stride. When Antonín Puč broke the deadlock in the 71st minute, it seemed that the football gods had tilted the evening in their favour. They stood on the verge of immortality.

And then came the moment.

With Italy pushing recklessly forward, the Czechs launched a counterattack. Jaroslav Bouček met the ball cleanly and struck it low towards the far corner. The Italian goalkeeper could only watch. The ball beat him, hit the inside of the post and appeared to land tantalizingly close to the goal line before being cleared. Had the referee awarded it, the score would have been 2–0, and the match beyond Italy's reach. The Czechoslovak players briefly lifted their arms in hope, then froze in disbelief. There were no video replays, no goal-line technology, no time to protest. The referee waved play on. The chance had gone.

As fate would have it, just minutes after the missed opportunity, Italy equalized through Raimundo Orsi. The psychological shift was as dramatic as the scoreline: Czechoslovakia, who moments earlier looked certain to be champions, appeared stunned. Italy, revived by survival, surged with new hunger. In extra time, Angelo Schiavio scored the winner, and history was written in blue rather than in Czechoslovak red and white.

Two World Cup Trophies

The 1934 FIFA World Cup carries an unusual distinction: two trophies were awarded to the winners. The coexistence of the original trophy (later renamed the Jules Rimet Trophy), FIFA's official symbol of global football supremacy, and the Coppa del Duce, a monumental prize commissioned by Benito Mussolini himself, reveals how deeply sport and politics intertwined in that tournament. If the World Cup was a stage, then the trophies were objects of symbolism – one universal, one ideological.

By 1934, the FIFA World Cup trophy was already a respected emblem. First introduced in 1930, it represented the organization's aspiration for unity through sport. Small, classical and elegant, featuring the figure of Nike, the Greek goddess of victory, it was designed to be passed from champion to champion, a legacy of footballing excellence. It was the prize that Czechoslovakia and Italy competed for on the pitch in the 1934 final in Rome.

Yet beside that stood something unprecedented. Mussolini commissioned a second trophy, known as the Coppa del Duce

(Cup of the Leader). This was a massive, towering and extravagant sculpture, much bigger than the official trophy, it reflected the fascist regime's love of grand display and its hunger to link political power to sporting triumph.

The ceremony after Italy's 2–1 victory over Czechoslovakia embodied this dual meaning. The Jules Rimet Trophy was handed to captain Gianpiero Combi as recognition of footballing achievement; the Coppa del Duce followed as recognition of national ideology. The players lifted both trophies, but the Coppa del Duce dominated the visual narrative in newspapers, stadium posters and official photographs. The state-controlled press ensured that images of Mussolini and the giant trophy circulated widely, elevating the sporting triumph into a triumph of the regime.

Over time, people seem to have forgotten the 'other trophy'. Like the regime that introduced it, the trophy too seemed to fade out of public memory.

QUIZ

Questions

Kick-Off

1. Most European nations declined to travel for the inaugural tournament in 1930, which was held in South America. What riposte from 1934 thus provides us with a unique anomaly in FIFA World Cup history?
2. On 25 March 1934, Italy defeated Greece 4–0 at the San Siro stadium in Milan. Anfilogino Guarisi, Giuseppe Meazza and Giovanni Ferrari scored, etching their names into the history books. Why was this game unique, and unlikely ever to be replicated ?
3. Which colonized side, which was later disbanded, played qualifying matches for the FIFA World Cup in 1934 and 1938? In 1934, they lost to Egypt, who went on to become the first African team ever to play the global tournament.

4. The 1934 World Cup featured no groups – the 16 participating teams faced each other in pre-quarterfinal knockout fixtures. What practice, now common in decisive preliminary-round games of global tournaments, was implemented for these eight matches?
5. When Austria and Germany faced off against one another in the third-place play-off, a peculiar problem arose – both teams had matching kits. To avoid confusion on the pitch, the referee ordered Austria to find an alternate uniform. And thus, at the Stadio Partenopeo, on 7 June, which illustrious club side's colours made a rather unique World Cup appearance?

Extra-Time

6. With just four non-European teams – Argentina, Brazil, Egypt and United States – travelling for the tournament, what record was created after the first round of matches? This feat had not occurred in 1930 and has never been repeated since.
7. From 1931 to 1934, Argentina had two regulatory bodies claiming to govern football in the country. As a result, different national leagues ran concurrently during this period. Primarily because of this, what selection anomaly occurred at this World Cup for Argentina – the reason many believe the usually strong side failed to advance beyond the opening round.
8. The hosts and eventual winners, Italy's opening fixture against Spain at this World Cup is often remembered for how ill-tempered it was. With multiple players being stretchered off, the game is often dubbed as the 'Battle of Florence'. What first is also credited to this fixture, a feature that has ceased to exist in recent times?
9. What commonality connects the names of the stadiums in Florence, Turin, Naples and Trieste used for this World Cup? Post the Second World War, widespread discontent paved the way for 'correction' and eventual renaming of these facilities. If it helps, the stadium in Rome that hosted the final could also tangentially make this list.

10. Angelo Schiavio and Edmund Conen both passed away in 1990, within a few months of each other. What 2006 ruling did they not live to see, one that relegated a feat of theirs from the 1934 World Cup?

Shoot-Out

11. The first African goalscorer in FIFA World Cup history, Abdelrahman Fawzy of Egypt, went on to become a successful and well-travelled coach. What feat of his was recently in the news as it was emulated by Brazilian Marcelinho Paraíba?
12. Developed in Central Europe in the 1920s and 30s, what style of football characterized by short passing, fluid movement and positional interchange and named because of a commonality that united the teams that developed it (Austria, Hungary, Czechoslovakia) was made popular at this World Cup?
13. The trip that wasn't! For any national team, travelling for a World Cup is momentous. Especially when air travel wasn't as prevalent as it is today, many had to endure long journeys to reach Italy for the tournament. Which national side, that had defeated Cuba in the preliminaries, had the misfortune of reaching Italy only to be eliminated from the tournament just three days before the start – after losing their final qualifier to the United States, who had only been invited very late to enter the qualifiers?
14. In the final, who equalized for the hosts with just nine minutes remaining. Accounts from onlookers and reports from newspapers back then suggested that it was a fluke, almost impossible shot that had managed to get in. To prove that it wasn't, this player returned to the pitch the next day in front of photographers.
15. Which 28-year-old from Sweden officiated both a semi-final and the final of the 1934 tournament? By doing the latter, he became – and still remains – the youngest referee of a FIFA World Cup final.

Word Search

Search this grid to name the eight quarter-finalists from the 1934 FIFA World Cup. If it helps, and as you would have read earlier in the quiz, this was the only time that all quarter-finalists came from the same continent – Europe.

N	A	D	E	C	N	X	L	O	G	B	W	C	Q	U	Q	A	O
N	U	N	A	K	C	E	A	R	H	O	I	I	G	O	L	H	Z
A	T	K	O	O	M	T	R	U	P	H	C	T	S	E	S	B	C
V	S	W	E	D	E	N	Y	A	S	V	D	A	D	D	P	T	G
I	H	J	V	M	U	I	T	I	X	T	E	L	D	U	A	M	E
F	M	K	T	P	Q	N	S	S	Y	M	R	Y	K	N	I	U	R
S	W	I	T	Z	E	R	L	A	N	D	G	I	C	S	N	Z	M
Z	H	U	N	G	A	R	Y	L	H	D	K	N	A	A	E	O	A
A	U	N	C	W	I	F	W	Z	P	S	U	O	G	E	L	K	N
O	P	L	C	Z	E	C	H	O	S	L	O	V	A	K	I	A	Y
S	U	L	Z	U	R	U	V	S	D	L	M	E	R	D	S	W	R
W	L	P	K	O	Q	N	Q	D	P	B	Y	O	M	H	D	J	S

Find the following words in the puzzle.
Words are hidden → and ↓ and ↘

CZECHOSLOVAKIA
SWITZERLAND
AUSTRIA
GERMANY
HUNGARY
SWEDEN
ITALY
SPAIN

ANSWER KEY

Answers to Questions

1. Uruguay refused to participate in 1934, making them the only defending champions to not contest the next edition.
2. This was the only instance of a host country playing a World Cup qualifier. (The hosts qualify to play the tournament automatically now.)
3. Mandatory Palestine
4. Simultaneous kick off (All teams played their first game at the exact same time at the 1934 World Cup.)
5. SSC Napoli
6. All eight quarter-finalists came from the same continent, Europe.
7. None of the players from Argentina's 1930 World Cup squad, which had finished as runners-up, were selected in 1934. They had all joined a league that was not recognized by the Argentine Football Association.
8. The first official replay of a World Cup match. (The initial game ended 1–1 and Italy won 1–0 in the return fixture).
9. The stadiums were named after Fascist leaders; following the fall of Fascism, they were renamed. (The stadium in Rome was called 'Stadium of the National Fascist Party'.)
10. In 2006, FIFA reviewed the goalscorers list from the early World Cups and awarded an extra goal to Oldřich Nejedlý, thus making him the sole winner of the Golden Boot from that edition. He had earlier shared that honour with Schiavio and Conen.
11. Managing two club sides simultaneously. He was in-charge of Zamalek FC and Ghazi El Mahalla in Egypt.
12. Danubian Style (The river Danube flowed through those countries.)
13. Mexico
14. Raimundo Orsi
15. Ivan Eklind

Solution to Word Search

```
. . . . . . . . . . . . . . . . . .
. . . . . . . A . . . . I . . . . .
. . . . . . . . U . . . T . . S . .
. S W E D E N . . S . . A . . P . G
. . . . . . . . . . T . L . . A . E
. . . . . . . . . . . R Y . . I . R
S W I T Z E R L A N D . I . . N . M
. H U N G A R Y . . . . . A . . . A
. . . . . . . . . . . . . . . . . N
. . . C Z E C H O S L O V A K I A Y
. . . . . . . . . . . . . . . . . .
. . . . . . . . . . . . . . . . . .
```

Word directions and start points are formatted: (Direction, X, Y)

CZECHOSLOVAKIA (E,4,10)
SWITZERLAND (E,1,7)
AUSTRIA (SE,8,2)
GERMANY (S,18,4)
HUNGARY (E,2,8)
SWEDEN (E,2,4)
ITALY (S,13,2)
SPAIN (S,16,3)

1938, FRANCE

STORIES

From Brazil to the World – The Bicycle Kick

The bicycle kick is an overhead kick in which the ball is struck mid-air while the player flips onto their back. It is one of football's most eye-catching skills. Over the years, many greats have used it to score outrageous-looking goals, but Leônidas da Silva, Brazil's hero from the 1938 World Cup, was among the earliest to perform and popularize it.

He is believed to have first used this kick in domestic football as early as 1932, during his time with the club Bonsucesso Futebol Clube.

During the 1938 World Cup, he attempted the move again against Czechoslovakia, and the effort stunned the European audience. Accounts of the game describe that the referee looked momentarily unsure whether such an acrobatic strike was permissible under the laws of the game.

While historians debate who truly 'invented' the bicycle kick (some trace it to Chile or Peru decades earlier), there is no doubt that Leônidas introduced it to the global audience.

Known to fans as the 'Black Diamond' and to teammates as the 'Rubber Man', outside of his acrobatic heroics too, Leônidas was simply unstoppable at the 1938 World Cup. He finished as the tournament's top scorer with 7 goals. His impact though went beyond just the number of times he found the back of the net.

In Brazil's Round of 16 match against Poland, played on a rain-soaked pitch in Strasbourg, he scored a hat-trick, scoring once in the first half and then adding two more in extra time to clinch a 6–5 win. Given the muddy field and reportedly having played through extra time with only one boot, accounts suggest this was one of the greatest single-game performances in the history of the tournament.

His team didn't win the tournament, finishing third, but Leônidas most certainly made the world see that there was different, almost more artistic way of playing the game – he perhaps embodied '*jogo bonito*', or play beautifully, before that phrase gained prominence.

Caribbean Representation

In 1938, Cuba qualified for the FIFA World Cup for the first and so far only time in its history. Much like other teams that would make the voyage across continents to participate in sporting events back then, the players boarded the USS *Orizaba* to reach France. Accounts suggest some from the squad had never left their island before and thus their journey across the Atlantic became part of their sporting folklore.

For weeks, the ship became their temporary stadium. Without a proper training ground, they improvised by passing the ball across wooden planks between lifeboats, juggling to keep balance against the waves and rehearsing movement patterns on a deck that swayed with the currents. Sea sickness and nausea turned out to be a major deterrent but in photographs and retellings, the players remembered the journey for the camaraderie they forged with one another.

Coming from an island that was still young as a footballing nation and where other sports were the prevalent pastimes, little was expected from the men who docked in Europe after weeks at sea. Yet their arrival symbolized something much larger. A team from the Caribbean had finally stepped onto football's grandest stage long before global expansion became the norm.

At the tournament itself, in their first match against Romania, the Cubans played with confidence, and despite falling behind, they fought back to force extra time in a match that finished 3–3.

Five days later, in the replay they won 2–1, stunning onlookers and reaching the quarter-finals. Sportswriters scrambled to find information about them. Who were these men? Which league did they play in? How had they trained? Few could imagine that their preparation had taken place not in pristine facilities, but on the rocking deck of USS *Orizaba*.

Their World Cup ended with an 8–0 loss to Sweden, the kind of result history tends to mock rather than understand. But in 1938, their journey symbolized something much bigger than just football; they had earned their right to be at a global footballing event and they were willing to go to any length to put their best show for it.

Pragmatism or Treason?

It is rather unfortunate that the story of Ernest Wilimowski, the first player ever to score 4 goals in a FIFA World Cup match, is not often remembered. A striker of staggering talent, whose brilliance at the 1938 World Cup impressed all, and yet, as the Second World War wreaked havoc, he faced resentment from his own countrymen.

Born in 1916 in Upper Silesia, a region that had shifted repeatedly between German and Polish control, Wilimowski scored goals with a sense of inevitability. From a teenager at Ruch Chorzów, he racked up numbers that seem almost too good to be true, and at the 1938 World Cup in France, he lived up to his promise.

In one of the most breathtaking matches the tournament has ever produced, Poland played Brazil in Strasbourg, and Wilimowski delivered a performance that is still spoken of with awe. On a pitch drowned in rain and mud, he scored four times – each time Brazil pulled ahead, he brought Poland back. The South Americans won 6–5, but the applause that followed Wilimowski as he walked off was for a man who had amazed everyone.

That match should have been the beginning of Wilimowski's global coronation. Instead, it became the peak of a life about to collapse. A year later, the Second World War began. His homeland,

Upper Silesia, was annexed into Nazi Germany, and its population was forced to adopt a fixed nationality. Wilimowski, like many around him became German overnight and eventually played for the German national team. What seemed as pragmatism to him, was seen as treason by others. And thus, in post-war Poland, a once-celebrated hero became a symbol of betrayal.

Polish authorities erased him from sporting memory. His records were stripped from books and his name vanished from official histories. Exile in Germany became permanent, and while he kept playing and scoring till he was in his forties, he never received the recognition his achievements might otherwise have warranted.

An Asian Pioneer

History often celebrates the champions, the record-breakers, and yet sometimes, the most profound stories belong not to the conquerors but to the explorers, those who chartered unfamiliar territory. Mo Heng Tan, the goalkeeper of the Dutch East Indies at the 1938 FIFA World Cup, was one such pioneer. His story is not merely that of a man who guarded the goal in his country's only World Cup appearance, but one that represents every youngster from a nation still under colonial rule, using sport to assert itself.

Born in February 1913, Mo Heng Tan was of ethnic Chinese descent, part of a community that would play a significant role in the early growth of football in the archipelago. At a time when identities in Southeast Asia were layered by colonial divisions, football created a shared space. Local clubs sprang up, attracting players regardless of ethnicity, and young Mo found his calling as a goalkeeper. He played for the club HCTNH Malang, and his rise to national selection reflects talent that commanded respect beyond the fragmented identity lines of the era.

In 1938, as the Dutch East Indies became the first team from Asia to qualify for the FIFA World Cup, football offered Mo Heng Tan and his teammates a rare escape from the world they knew – a chance to stand on even footing with Europe and South America's elites, not as the colonized but as competitors. Their journey to France took them across continents by ship and train, and although their only match of the tournament ended in a 6–0 defeat, their presence represented something bigger.

After 1938, much of Mo Heng Tan's life receded into obscurity, as did that of many of his teammates. Yet his legacy continued in quiet ways. He is the only recorded player from that World Cup squad who was later documented to having played for an Indonesian side after independence, taking part in a match in Singapore in 1951. In a period when the new republic was still navigating identity and sovereignty, seeing a man from the 1938 squad still wearing the colours of Indonesia helped bridge the colonial past to a new national story.

The Falling Shorts

The 1938 World Cup semi-final between Italy and Brazil in Marseille carried enormous weight. The defending champions, Italy, were one match away from returning to the final, while Brazil, without the brilliant Leônidas, who was injured and resting, were trying to reach their first ever final. Tension was palpable, but in the middle of the seriousness, a moment occurred that would become one of the World Cup's most enduring and comedic legends – the story of Giuseppe Meazza's falling shorts.

Perhaps the biggest star of football from that era, Italy's Giuseppe Meazza, who later had the iconic San Siro stadium renamed in his honour, stepped up to take a penalty in the second half. As he jogged towards the spot, something unexpected happened: the elastic of his shorts snapped. His shorts began to slip downward, but he remained unfazed and did not panic. He simply placed one hand on his hips, used the other hand to hold up his shorts, and prepared to take the penalty with the nonchalance of a man tying his shoe.

The referee reportedly asked if he wished to adjust his kit. Meazza shook his head. He would take the kick exactly as he was.

And so, holding his shorts in place with one hand, he ran up on a short diagonal, struck the ball cleanly with his right foot, and sent the Brazilian goalkeeper the wrong way. Italy went 2–0 up, eventually winning 2–1 and reaching the final, where they defeated Hungary to become back-to-back World Cup champions.

QUIZ

Questions

Kick-Off

1. What distinction was Italy bestowed with for the 1938 World Cup, paving way for a custom that remained in place until the 2002 edition in South Korea and Japan?
2. Which iconic coach led Italy to its second consecutive World Cup trophy at this edition, thus becoming the only one to win two World Cups as well as an Olympic gold medal (at the 1936 Berlin Games)?
3. Which then colonized nation became the first team from Asia to play in the World Cup? Having received byes/ walkovers in the qualification rounds against Japan and the United States, they ended up playing only one game in France, a 0–6 loss to Hungary and have to date never qualified for the World Cup again.
4. The original number of entries for the 1938 World Cup was 16. However, when the tournament started on 4 June, only 15 teams competed – Sweden received a walkover in their game and progressed automatically to the quarter-finals. What non-footballing reason caused this?
5. Making their first and, so far, only appearance at the FIFA World Cup, which Caribbean team made it to the quarter-final stage at this tournament? In their first match, they played Romania and drew 3–3, but won the replay 2–1. They then advanced to the quarter-finals, where they lost 0–8 to Sweden.

Extra-Time

6. Named after the former French rugby player Yves du Manoir, what distinction did the venue of the 1938 World Cup final achieve, one that the iconic Wembley Stadium is often credited with? For additional context, the other stadiums that make this fascinating list include the Maracanã in Rio de Janeiro, the Stadio Olimpico in Rome and the Olympiastadion in Berlin.
7. Ottorino Barassi was an Italian administrator who first helped organize the 1934 World Cup and then the 1950 edition in Brazil. A respected member of the ecosystem, what did he do post the 1938 tournament and during the Second World War which has iconized his stature in the history of the World Cup?
8. Hungarian stalwart György Sárosi had a spectacular tournament, scoring 5 goals in total. What record did he set at this edition of the World Cup, one that is so rare that it has only been emulated twice since?
9. Gino Colaussi was one of those understated heroes of the Italian team who retained the World Cup in 1938. A Triestina forward, what first did he achieve at the final of this edition, one that has been repeated by modern greats like Zinedine Zidane, Ronaldo and Lionel Messi and bettered by Geoff Hurst and Kylian Mbappé?
10. With substitutions still not allowed, what was the name of the French captain who scored against Italy in the quarter-final and got injured in the same sequence? He limped for the rest of the match and effectively played on one leg, as France became the first ever hosts to not lift the World Cup.

Shoot-Out

11. Established primarily as an open-air velodrome, which iconic facility, that hosted the opening game of the 1938 World Cup, was used as the finishing point of Tour de France when it was initiated in July 1903?

12. Known as the *maglia nera*, what was used by the Italian team at least once at this edition, in their game against the hosts? Ordered by the regime of Benito Mussolini, it seemed to be a direct reference to their paramilitary force that lay at the core of Italy's fascist movement.
13. When FIFA devised the World Cup, South American countries were under the impression that the hosting rights would alternate between South America and Europe after Uruguay hosted in 1930 and Italy in 1934. Thus, when the 1938 tournament was awarded to France – another European host – they were unhappy and threatened to boycott the tournament.

    Historical accounts suggest one country was particularly disgruntled – they had expected to host, and though FIFA offered them a last-minute slot in the play-offs, they couldn't make the tournament owing to travel expenses as well a growing internal rift. Which team was this?
14. Labelled the 'Battle of Bordeaux', the quarter-final between Czechoslovakia and Brazil played on 12 June was ill-tempered with multiple players being carried off with injuries. What distinctive 'last' in World Cup history did this game provide us with?
15. In the same quarter-final, Zezé Procópio, Arthur Machado and Jan Říha missed part of the game despite not getting injured/stretched off. This left fans perplexed – what had happened, a solution to which wasn't found till as late as the 1970 edition in Mexico?

Anagrams

Including the head coach, there were five members of the Italian squad who won both the 1934 and the 1938 editions, giving them the distinction of being the first multiple winners of the FIFA World Cup. Unscramble the following to find their names:

1. DOUGIMITATES
2. ADEGERONIMOZOLL
3. IRVOTTOZIPZOO
4. AARENFIRINGIVOR
5. EMUSPAGEPIAZZE

ANSWER KEY

Answers to Questions

1. They were the first defending champions to qualify automatically for the next World Cup – since 2006, even the previous winners need to qualify.
2. Vittorio Pozzo
3. Dutch East Indies
4. After qualification was complete, Anschluss united Austria with Germany. As a result, Austria did not participate in the tournament (with some of their players playing for the unified German team).
5. Cuba
6. It is the first stadium to host the Olympics and the World Cup final.
7. He hid the Jules Rimet World Cup Trophy in a shoebox at his home to save it from the Nazi troops during the Second World War.
8. He scored in every game he played in – only Just Fontaine (in 1958) and Jairzinho (in 1970) have achieved the same.
9. He was the first to score 2 goals in a World Cup final.
10. Oscar Heisserer
11. Parc de Princes
12. All-black kits (a nod to the Blackshirts, the regime's paramilitary organization). *Maglia nera* quite literally means 'black jersey' or 'black shirt'.
13. Argentina

14. Last replay in a FIFA World Cup
15. Verbal red cards – referees used to simply walk up to players and inform them that they were excluded from a game; it was only in 1970 that the card system was implemented.

Solutions to Anagrams

1. Guido Masetti
2. Eraldo Monzeglio
3. Vittorio Pozzo
4. Giovanni Ferrari
5. Guiseppe Meazza

1950, BRAZIL

STORIES

Heartbreak in Front of a Record Crowd

On 16 July 1950, the newly built Maracanã Stadium rose like a concrete colossus over Rio de Janeiro, ready to witness what Brazilians believed would be a national coronation.

Nearly 2,00,000 spectators, the largest crowd ever to attend a football game, seemed assured of the hosts securing either a draw or a win, which would have helped them clinch the World Cup. Dailies in Rio de Janeiro had already pre-printed news of them winning, and as the game started, the hosts, buoyed by the overwhelming support as well as riding a rich vein of form, attacked with the confidence of a side fulfilling its destiny.

Three minutes into the second half, the Maracanã reached its expected eruption. Friaça, charging down the right, sent a low shot past the Uruguayan goalkeeper. The stadium vibrated with relief as much as joy. Triumph was now imminent.

And yet, it wasn't meant to be.

As the Brazilians were celebrating the goal, opposing skipper Obdulio Varela's leadership carved its legend. He deliberately walked the length of the pitch to protest the goal, later admitting that he had not hoped to overturn it, but to offset Brazilian momentum and steady his own team. Holding the ball, he allowed the roar to subside and then spoke to his team.

From that moment, Uruguay's resolve hardened. In the 66th minute, winger Alcides Ghiggia, elusive all afternoon, darted down the right before slipping a pass inside to Juan Alberto Schiaffino. Schiaffino's finish was crisp and ruthless, flying beyond goalkeeper Moacir Barbosa. The Maracanã fell into a silence so total it seemed to vacuum the air from the stadium. Brazil were still champions with a draw and all was not lost.

But thirteen minutes later, that changed – Ghiggia surged again past the exposed left flank and shot past Barbosa to hand Uruguay their second World Cup and the whole of Brazil, a heartbreak.

Joe Gaetjens and the Miracle on Grass

On a cool afternoon in Belo Horizonte on 29 June 1950, football produced one of its most enduring legends – a result so improbable that journalists refused to believe the scoreline. At the centre of it stood Joe Gaetjens, a Haitian-born, part-time dishwasher from New York, whose single, glancing touch created what came to be known as the 'Miracle on Grass'.

Gaetjens was not your typical superstar. Born in Port-au-Prince, he moved to the United States to study accounting, taking up a dishwashing job in a Manhattan restaurant to support himself. He played football part-time for Brookhattan in the American Soccer League, a competition largely overlooked even within the country. His selection to the US national team wasn't a certainty and yet, there he was.

His – and the United States' – opponent that day, from across the Atlantic, England, arrived at the 1950 World Cup as self-appointed masters of the game. This was their first World Cup appearance, and their squad featured stars like Billy Wright, Tom Finney and Stanley Matthews. To most observers, the match against the United States seemed less like a contest and more like a formality.

Yet sport has a unique way of defying prediction, and the United States, running on adrenaline and defiant energy, chased every ball. England, complacent and strangely disjointed, failed to convert early chances. And in the 38th minute came the moment that changed the match – and Joe Gaetjens' life.

A cross shot from American midfielder Walter Bahr skidded across the grass. It was not powerful, and England's goalkeeper, Bert Williams, appeared ready to collect it. But Gaetjens, streaking across the box, flung himself forward and flicked the ball with the faintest glance of his head. That deflection, subtle but precise, redirected the ball just out of Williams' reach and into the far corner.

Riding on that effort, the final score read United Stated 1–0 England; Brazilian newspapers assumed a typographical error. In an age before instant communication, it took some time for the world to know, and to understand, what had happened in Belo Horizonte that day.

Gaetjens became an overnight sensation. Yet fame faded quickly. He returned to a modest career, later moving back to Haiti, where his story took a tragic turn. In 1964, during the Duvalier dictatorship, Gaetjens was arrested for suspected political ties and disappeared, never to be seen again. There is no account of his death or where he might be buried – a sad end to a life that, even if for a day, lived through a miracle.

Italy's Voyage of Sorrow and Survival

Twice defending champion Italy's journey to the 1950 World Cup is inseparable from a tragedy that remains one of the darkest days in sports history: the Superga air disaster of 1949. That catastrophe reshaped Italian football, altered the course of their World Cup campaign and forced them into an odyssey by sea that symbolized both mourning and determination.

On 4 May 1949, the plane carrying the legendary Torino team, which had dominated Italian football after the Second World War, crashed into the Basilica of Superga outside Turin. All 31 people aboard were killed. Torino had won five consecutive Serie A titles and supplied the core of the national team, a golden generation whose brilliance had been expected to lead Italy into a new era.

When preparations began for the 1950 World Cup, the wounds were still painfully fresh, and flying through the same skies that had taken their compatriots was too painful. The football federation thus, along with the players, united in one sentiment – that they would not fly.

Instead, they Italian team, the Azzurri (the Blues), boarded the SS *Sises*, a passenger ship that would take them on a 16-day voyage across the Atlantic. The contrast with other teams who flew in modern aircraft and trained upon arrival could not have been starker. Italy's journey was slow and grim; players slept in cramped cabins, sharing stories of fallen teammates, sometimes crying, sometimes laughing in remembrance. Evenings were heavy with melancholy. Crew members later recalled that the team kept to themselves, united in grief.

By the time they arrived in Brazil, they were physically drained and emotionally stretched. Their preparation had been inadequate with the memory of Superga lingering over every match. They played only two games, winning only one game against Paraguay and were eliminated in the group stage.

Perhaps the results weren't the most important measure that year. Simply being present at the World Cup, for the Azzurri, was a tribute to the memory of Torin – a statement of resilience after unimaginable heartbreak.

The Unlikely Heroes from Scandinavia

In 1950, Swedish football was governed by a strictly amateur policy. Any player who turned professional abroad was automatically barred from the national team and thus Sweden travelled to Brazil without their three greatest talents: Gunnar Gren, Gunnar Nordahl and Nils Liedholm, the trio famously referred to as Gre-No-Li, who had just transformed AC Milan. The absence of these legends left many believing Sweden would struggle even to compete.

The squad that was assembled was composed largely of everyday men with ordinary professions. Some worked in factories, others in offices; many trained in the evenings after work. They lacked the glamour and notoriety of rivals like Brazil or England.

However, their opening match against reigning world champions Italy set the tone for what turned out to be a memorable campaign. Italy, still grieving the loss of the Grande Torino team from the Superga disaster, were taken aback by Sweden's tactical play and eventually went down 2–3.

Next, against Paraguay, they produced one of the tournament's most impressive performances, earning a thrilling 2–2 draw. The match highlighted the brilliance of squad's emerging stars: the lone eligible Nordahl brother, midfielder Knut Nordahl; the finishing prowess of Karl-Erik Palmér; and of course goalkeeper Kalle Svensson, who anchored a defence that played with admirable composure against far more fancied teams.

Sweden's final standing of third place was rightly perceived as one of that World Cup's finest showings. For a squad full of amateurs, without its brightest stars, it was a remarkable overachievement.

India's Reluctance to Travel for a World Cup

When the 1950 World Cup opened in Brazil, it marked football's return after a 12-year hiatus caused by a global war. Among the names on the qualified list was a surprising entrant: India. Their presence drew curiosity from around the world, for India had earned their place not through traditional qualification but because several Asian and Middle Eastern teams had withdrawn. India, which had gained political independence just three years earlier, ultimately never travelled for the event.

The reasons behind this decision have, over time, become clouded by myth, most famously the claim that India was banned from playing barefoot. The truth, however, is far more layered, reflecting administrative confusion, financial strain and differing sporting priorities.

The most widely repeated explanation is that India withdrew because FIFA insisted players wear boots. It is true that many

Indian footballers of the era preferred to play barefoot, having achieved success in domestic and international tournaments without footwear. The image of India as a barefoot, romantic underdog has endured in global memory, in part because of the dramatic visual contrast it offered. Yet historical records show that an outright ban on playing barefoot was never imposed; rather, the rule requiring boots had been established in 1948 for player safety. Moreover, the All India Football Federation never cited this as the primary reason for withdrawal. The barefoot story, though evocative, oversimplifies a much more complex reality.

The real obstacles were largely financial and logistical. Travelling from India to Brazil in 1950 was an expensive undertaking, far beyond the federations's modest means. FIFA offered to cover accommodation but not travel, and even subsidized tickets exceeded their budget.

Another significant factor was India's prioritization of the Olympics over the World Cup. In the mid-twentieth century, many countries saw the Olympics as the pinnacle of amateur sport. India's football administration valued the Olympic stage more than FIFA's tournament, which was still gaining global prestige. Indeed, India prepared diligently for the 1948 Olympics in London, where their spirited performance earned admiration despite losing 2–1 to France.

The World Cup, by comparison, did not seem as essential or glamorous, and thus the opportunity was passed. Sadly, the team has since never come close to qualifying for the tournament.

QUIZ

Questions

Kick-Off

1. What unique first – and so far only – World Cup occurrence did then host Brazil, along with past and future hosts Sweden, Spain

and Uruguay contribute to, at the 1950 edition of the tournament?

2. In their group game against Switzerland, Mexico wore a jersey with vertical blue and white stripes. As both teams had shown up for the game in similar colours, which local club team's help was sought to ensure a different-looking kit was worn by the Central-American team?
3. Which European powerhouse withdrew from the tournament last minute citing long hours of travel between host cities, and thus reducing a group to just two teams – with Uruguay then playing Bolivia in what was a straight knockout and advancing to the final stage?
4. As was the case with the other early editions of the tournament, there were mythical accounts galore from 1950 edition as well. The United States vs England game provided quite a few such stories, including claims that the Americans took rum shots before leaving their hotel for the game. However, what on-field anomaly did their goalkeeper Frank Borghi indulge in? He later credited the same for his heroic performance, as his team went on to upset the English.
5. Before Brazil's match against Spain, a fan famously carried a piece of furniture painted with the Spanish flag, symbolizing Brazil's intention to 'finish' their opponents. Later, he returned for the Uruguay match carrying the same item painted in Uruguay's colours, only to abandon it in the stands after the shock defeat. What item was this, perhaps indicative of bringing a team's reign at the event?

Extra-Time

6. This Brazilian goalkeeper was unfairly blamed for the 1950 defeat and carried the stigma for decades. Years later, in despair, he removed a piece of the original Maracanã goalpost used in the final, took it home and eventually burnt it, hoping to rid himself of the 'curse' that followed him throughout his life. It did not, and he later remarked, shortly before his death, *'In Brazil, the*

maximum prison sentence is 30 years. My sentence has lasted 50.' What was his name?

7. From the opening whistle of the game between United States and Chile, everyone realized the match was going to be a spectacle of survival rather than skill. The ball refused to roll, every pass dying in a puddle. Players who attempted to sprint ended up sliding several metres like children on a slip-and-slide. Some later commented that it felt like playing water polo while standing. What moniker, an ode to these conditions, was thus given to this game?
8. What rare distinction did Alfred Bickel of Switzerland and Erik Nilsson of Sweden achieve at the 1950 World Cup?
9. Which South American team, appearing in their second World Cup, again failed to win a point? It was not until their next appearance in 1994 that they managed a positive result, thus ending a point-less drought of 64 years at the global meet.
10. For the 1950 World Cup, FIFA created a Southeast Asian qualifying group. Three of the four teams that were invited withdrew from the qualifiers paving the way for India to receive a direct spot despite not playing any matches. Ironically, they too declined to travel to Brazil, meaning that no Asian team ultimately featured at the tournament. Which three teams had initially withdrawn from the qualifiers?

Shoot-Out

11. After the disappointment of losing a World Cup at home, what ritual did Brazil discontinue after the tournament, as the nation, grieving through sport, was deemed in need of a visual rebirth. If it helps, the replacement was ideated by Aldyr Garcia Schlee, a teenager from Pelotas.
12. Africa saw no participants at this edition too. It is believed that Egypt – the only independent country from the continent and a FIFA member – needing to play qualifiers against either teams

from Europe or Asia to reach the World Cup made it trickier. There were no other African teams to play qualifiers against till the 1938 edition. For 1950 though, which other African country (still under colonial rule) was a member of FIFA and had an opportunity to play in the tournament, but chose not to field a team?

13. George Graham, chairman of the Scottish Football Association, declared before the qualification competition, that Scotland would go to Brazil only as winners of a specific championship that they had competed in. As luck would have it, they ended up in second place, and despite their captain George Young's repeated pleas, Graham stood firm on his decision. What tournament was this, the first ever in international football to serve as a FIFA World Cup qualifier for 1950 as well as 1954?
14. To commemorate 25 years of the onset of a significant chapter in its history, what decision did the FIFA Congress take in Luxembourg in July 1946?
15. What was unique about Uruguay's Víctor Rodríguez Andrade, one of the stars of their triumphant 1950 side? Him featuring in the champions' line-up ensured a World Cup first that has been emulated only twice since.

Crossword

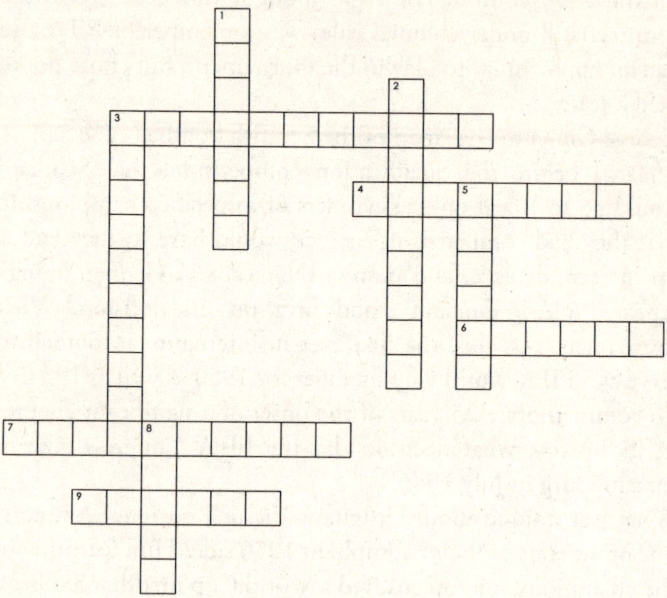

Across: →

3. Qualified without playing a game
4. Goalkeeper who played in 5 World Cups
6. Northernmost city to host this tournament
7. Only team from Eastern Europe
9. Fond of books! Also a referee

Down: ↓

1. Coach of Uruguay
2. Stadium in São Paulo
3. First goalscorer in final for Uruguay
5. Barcelona striker who scored 4 goals
8. Fourth Place Finishers

ANSWER KEY

Answers to Questions

1. They competed in a final round-robin tournament (each team played the others once to determine the World Cup champions) – this is the only such instance.
2. Esporte Clube Cruzeiro from Porto Alegre
3. France
4. He played with no gloves because he believed that 'they softened his hands'!
5. Coffin (as Brazil tried to 'bury' their opponents)
6. Moacir Barbosa
7. Battle of the Mud
8. They played in World Cup final before and after the Second World War (in 1938 and 1950).
9. Bolivia
10. Indonesia, Philippines and Burma
11. The blue-and-white jersey; they started wearing their iconic yellow-and-blue jerseys soon after.
12. Sudan
13. Home Championship, played between teams from England, Scotland, Wales and Ireland
14. Renamed the World Cup trophy after its then president, Jules Rimet. (It was in 1921 that he was elected to this position.)
15. He was the nephew of José Andrade, a member of Uruguay's 1930 World Cup winning side. Together, they became the first relatives to win the World Cup – a feat later emulated by two sets of brothers: Fritz and Ottmar Walter (West Germany, 1954) and Jack and Bobby Charlton (England, 1966).

Solution to Crossword

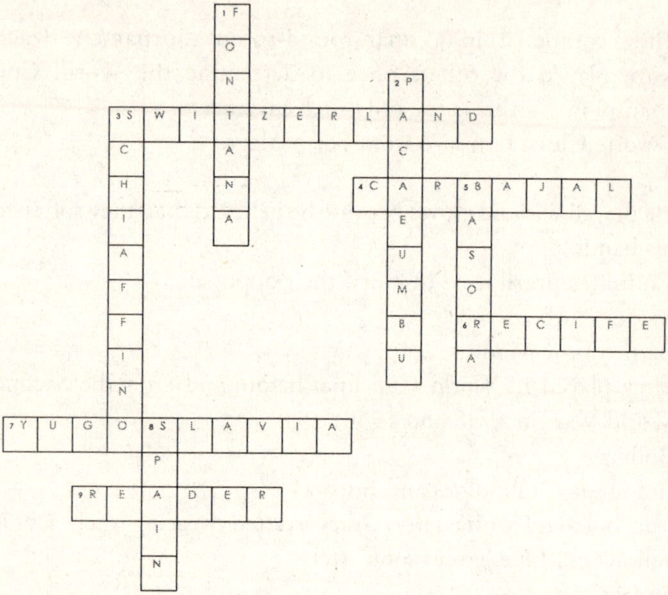

Across: →

3. Qualified without playing a game
4. Goalkeeper who played in 5 World Cups
6. Northernmost city to host this tournament
7. Only team from Eastern Europe
9. Fond of books! Also a referee

Down: ↓

1. Coach of Uruguay
2. Stadium in São Paulo
3. First goalscorer in final for Uruguay
5. Barcelona striker who scored 4 goals
8. Fourth Place Finishers

1954, SWITZERLAND

STORIES

A Group Stage Like No Other

The group stage of the 1954 FIFA World Cup was held in a unique format. Like later editions of the tournament, it saw 16 teams divided into four groups. However, each team played only two group matches, not three.

This was due to a seeding process intended to ensure that the stronger teams in each group would not routinely play each other. Each group contained two seeded and two unseeded teams, with fixtures arranged unevenly between them. This meant that a group could contain two giants who might not meet at all, while weaker teams bore the brunt of facing both. Teams could thus qualify or be eliminated without ever facing the strongest side in their group. Hungary and West Germany, both placed in the same group, played each other only once in the group stage, and knowing that the result would not be decisive for qualification, the latter fielded a weakened team. The idea of a 'true table' reflecting relative strength was effectively abandoned.

Even more bizarre was the method for separating teams level on points after the group stage. Goal difference was irrelevant. A win by a larger margin counted no more than a 1–0 victory. Instead, ties were resolved by play-offs, which were scheduled after the group stage. The teams who contested these also had to deal with fatigue, disrupted recovery, and an added element of randomness into what was supposed to be an orderly phase of the competition. Former two-time world champions, Italy, were eliminated this way.

It was so disorderly that accounts suggest that even journalists at the time struggled to explain qualification scenarios to readers. Even players admitted they never fully understood the system.

Thankfully, better sense prevailed, and the format was abandoned for good after this edition.

The Kick That Won the World Cup

Going into the 1954 World Cup, Hungary was the best team in the world. They were the reigning Olympic champions and had set foot in Switzerland for the tournament on the back of a 32-game unbeaten run.

At the forefront of their surge to the zenith of the sport was their captain and charismatic striker, Ferenc Puskás. Nicknamed the 'Galloping Major' for having served in the army, he was expected to dominate the World Cup, kicking off with two goals in his nation's 9–0 rout of South Korea in their opening match.

They next faced West Germany, and it was in that game that, while the Mighty Magyars, as they were nicknamed, were 5–1 up, Puskás was tackled by Werner Liebrich, which sent him crashing down. The Hungarians maintain that the centre-half attacked their captain after he no longer had the ball, while the German captain, Fritz Walter later recalled that it was a fair tackle, but that Puskás landed awkwardly. Regardless of its nature, it was a pivotal moment in the tournament, one that Brian Glanville later called 'the kick that won the World Cup'.

Puskás still managed to play a part in the quarter-final against Brazil but was clearly struggling. His ankle was closely monitored, with early X-rays showing his left ankle's main ligament nearly severed, making him miss the semi-final. Not one to let go of an opportunity to lead his team to a World Cup, he went against the advice of doctors and decided to play in the final.

He even scored after six minutes in the final in Bern as his team took the lead. However, his inclusion seemed to have disrupted the rhythm of the side, which had won the previous game; winger Lazlo Budai was dropped for the final, thus reshuffling the other wingers and forcing them into unfamiliar roles. The team clearly struggled, and by half-time, saw their lead being nullified.

In the second half, West Germany took the lead for the first time. Puskás, beleaguered and guarded by Liebrich, who had inflicted the tackle in the group stage, was now a pale shadow of his mighty self. With two minutes to go, he did score to equalize, but was deemed offside, and thus, against all odds, West Germany won the World Cup. And they owed that to the pivotal tackle weeks earlier.

Captain's War Cry

Herbert Zimmermann, served in the Second World War as a captain, was honoured with a Knight's Cross and yet, millions across Germany remember him only by his voice.

On 4 July 1954, Zimmermann, who had by then transitioned into being a commentator, expected that his day at the office, working on the World Cup final, would involve narrating to millions of listeners on West German radio, one Hungarian goal after another. The Magical Magyars had, after all, demolished them 8–3 in the group stage and were on a world-record unbeaten run.

Eight minutes in, and Zimmermann had already narrated two Hungarian goals. He too had conceded defeat and, by later accounts, was hoping that his country could keep the margin down. West Germany didn't give up, though, and fought back to level the score in just 12 minutes.

Over the next hour, both teams tried hard to take the lead but failed. Eventually, in the 84th minute, the ball fell to Helmut Rahn.

'Rahn shoots! Goal! Goal! Goal! Goal!' Zimmermann exclaimed, losing his voice as he tried to take in what had just happened.

With people across West Germany frantically checking to see if they had been disconnected, the legendary commentator finally regained his composure and concluded: 'Goal for Germany! Germany lead 3–2. Call me mad, call me crazy!'

Till today, it remains one of football's most iconic narrations!

Battle of Berne

Not all football classics are instantly recognized as era-defining. The 1954 FIFA World Cup quarter-final between Hungary and Brazil, played on 27 June at Bern's Wankdorf Stadium, did not initially seem destined for such historical weight. Yet, with time, 'The Battle of Berne' has become iconic, marking both the last great hurrah of Hungary's Golden Team and the final, painful lesson before Brazil ascended to footballing supremacy.

Hungary entered the tournament as the dominant force of early-1950s football. Led by stars such as Sándor Kocsis, Nándor Hidegkuti, Zoltán Czibor and the legendary Ferenc Puskás, the 'Mighty Magyars' were reigning Olympic champions and unbeaten in 32 games. Their superiority was proven in famous victories, none greater than their 6–3 dismantling of England at Wembley in 1953. In Switzerland, they continued their dominance with emphatic wins over Korea Republic (9–0) and West Germany (8–3).

Brazil, by contrast, was still healing from the trauma of the 1950 World Cup, when a shock defeat to Uruguay at the Maracanã Stadium robbed them of a title they believed was already theirs. The response was a transformation: new players, a new coach and even a new identity marked by the now-iconic yellow jersey. With talents like Didi and Nilton Santos, they progressed from the group stage, motivated by the chance to erase past humiliation. Yet this confidence slid into complacency with coach Zezé Moreira even dismissing the significance of Puskás's absence.

Hungary immediately exposed that misjudgement. Within seven minutes, Hidegkuti and Kocsis put them 2–0 ahead. Brazil pulled one back through Djalma Santos from the penalty spot, but another Hungarian penalty restored the advantage. Julinho's fine strike brought Brazil hope but then the game descended into chaos.

Tempers erupted as fierce challenges escalated into outright violence. Nilton Santos and Bozsik were dismissed after a brawl; desperate defending turned into reckless aggression. Humberto's brutal foul and subsequent red card left Brazil down to nine men. Kocsis sealed Hungary's 4–2 victory late on but the final whistle did not end the hostilities. Fighting spread from the pitch to the tunnel and even outside the stadium, ensuring the match would be remembered more for chaos than brilliance.

Referee Arthur Ellis later lamented that he simply hoped the game would finish.

In an era where substitutions were not allowed and there were no cards handed out as punishment for disorderly behaviour, the Battle of Berne became the stand out reference for how disorderly things could get if things went out of control.

Captain, Leader, Legend

On a rain-soaked afternoon in Bern, a soft-spoken captain led West Germany into a World Cup final that the world believed they had no right to reach. His name was Fritz Walter. His journey from the shadows of war to the zenith of sport would become the emotional heartbeat of a tournament that helped restore dignity and hope to a broken nation.

Years before he ever lifted a trophy, Walter was simply a survivor. Drafted during the Second World War, he carried the weight of conflict across Europe. He contracted malaria during his service, an illness that would leave his body sensitive to heat for the rest of his life. On grey and rainy days, however, he felt strong again. His teammates thus called such weather 'Fritz-Walter-

Wetter', or 'Fritz Walter weather', conditions made for their captain's courage.

His survival itself was a matter of chance. Near the war's end, he was captured and faced a future of brutal imprisonment in a Soviet camp. But one guard recognized him from the football fields of pre-war Europe. That moment of recognition spared his life. It also gave Walter something powerful: the knowledge that people still recognized him because of football and that life after war still had a purpose.

By 1954, West Germany was taking its first steps back towards the international community. Still scarred, still stigmatized, the nation's footballers were viewed as outsiders. Expectations were negligible. The team was inexperienced, yet Walter remained steady. At 33, he led not with speeches, but with belief. His teammates trusted him because he never wavered.

Then came the final: West Germany vs Hungary. The Mighty Magyars arrived unbeaten in 32 matches, the greatest force football had ever known. But as clouds gathered and rain began to fall, Walter smiled to himself. This was his weather.

Hungary surged ahead 2–0 inside ten minutes. Yet Walter refused to allow panic to grow. He walked calmly among his teammates, reminding them of who they were becoming. Step by step, West Germany fought back to equalize. And then, with the match drifting into its decisive moments, Helmut Rahn struck a goal that shook the world.

When the final whistle blew on what would be called 'The Miracle of Berne', Fritz Walter fell to the turf in triumph. It brought hope to a country that was still healing.

'It wasn't just for us,' Walter later said. 'It was for the people who needed to believe again.'

He lifted the trophy gently, almost humbly. The hero who had survived war and illness asked for no spotlight. He returned home to Kaiserslautern, the only club he represented.

QUIZ

Questions

Kick-Off

1. What unique rule used at this edition of the World Cup ensured fewer draws in the group stage (just three draws in 16 matches)?
2. Three countries made their debut at the 1954 edition. While Turkey and Scotland had both been invited in 1950 too but later withdrew, which was the third team, from Asia, that became the first independent country from the continent to play the World Cup?
3. The 16 teams were divided into four groups of four teams each at this edition of the World Cup, a structure that later became the norm for decades. The matches, however, were scheduled in a unique format, generally designed to/largely intended to pit a seeded team against an unseeded team, ensuring some teams never played one another despite being in the same group. What other group-stage anomaly did this structure result in, with Italy and Turkey on at the receiving end of what many would deem an unfair elimination?
4. Sándor Kocsis of Hungary had a dream tournament, scoring a then record 11 goals in just five matches. What goalscoring feat was he the first to achieve, one that has only been emulated by Just Fontaine of France in 1958 and Gerd Muller of West Germany in 1970?
5. Given the geographical ambiguity of one of their opponents, how is West Germany's win at this tournament unique in FIFA World Cup history?

Extra-Time

6. The final match between West Germany and Hungary, known as the 'Miracle of Bern', was played in heavy rain.

The pitch became increasingly muddy, making conditions difficult, and at half-time, with the score tied 2–2, the German manager, Sepp Herberger, famously ordered a crucial adjustment. This was carried out by an entrepreneur who was working closely with the team. Who was he, and what change did he make that gave the West German team a crucial advantage in the second half, widely credited as a major factor in their unexpected 3–2 victory over the heavily favoured 'Mighty Magyars', the Hungarians, who had been unbeaten for four years?

7. The Meiji Jingu Gaien Stadium has a special place in sporting history. As the venue for the 1930 Far Eastern Games, it remained the marquee facility in Japan leading up to, and well beyond, the Second World War, and was eventually demolished to make space for the National Stadium, which has hosted both the 1964 as well as the 2020 Summer Olympics (held in 2021 owing to the COVID–19 pandemic). How did it make its way into World Cup history in 1954 though?
8. Literally meaning 'Hard Tower' and used in the 1954 edition, in which city was the Hardturm Stadium located – a city that has become the epicenter of the World Cup football movement?
9. In a bizarre move, teams were seeded for the tournament before qualification had even concluded. While most teams who were tipped to do well made it to Switzerland, which European side suffered the ignominious fate of being the only seeded team to not make it to the World Cup?
10. How did a young teenager called Luigi Franco Gemma, whose father worked in a stadium in Rome, contribute to the 1954 World Cup?

Shoot-Out

11. The *folha seca* or 'dry leaf' is a legendary free-kick technique where the ball drifts and suddenly dips before hitting the net. Which Brazilian great, who first shone on the world stage at the World Cup in 1954, was the pioneer of this?
12. Between 1952 and 1956, Andy Beattie was in charge of Huddersfield Town, and yet he was invited to coach Scotland for the 1954 World Cup. After their first game, a 0–1 loss to Austria, Beattie resigned mid-tournament. When he got back to his club, which manager, and a former teammate of his, was appointed as his assistant as he neared the end of an illustrious coaching career?
13. South Korea's journey to compete at the 1954 World Cup was quite something. The squad first travelled by train from Seoul to Busan, where they boarded a ship for Japan. In Tokyo, when they found that the plane wasn't large enough, the team decided to split into two groups and take separate routes to reach Switzerland. If one of the transit points was Bangkok (nine players), which other South Asian city did the other members of the team transit through?
14. Which future administrator and politician captained Italy at this World Cup? One of the most capped players for Juventus, he later served as the clubs' CEO and chairman, and from 1994 to the turn of the millennium, was a deputy to the European Parliament.
15. England, competing in their second World Cup, conceded 4 goals twice – first against Belgium, then against Uruguay in the quarter-finals. Who was their right-back, an iconic player who would become instrumental in building a robust defence for a famous triumph a few years later?

Connect

Group the 16 words into four groups of four. Each group shares something in common. Each word belongs to one group only.

KOCSIS	WANKDORF	HIDEGKUTI	PUSKÁS
HÜGI	LEATHER	ZURICH	STUDS
RAIN	BERN	RAHN	WALTER
ADIDAS	WAGNER	PROBST	HARDTURM

ANSWER KEY

Answers to Questions

1. If a game finished level after 90 minutes; extra time of 30 minutes was played. The match was declared a draw only if the teams remained tied after this additional period.
2. South Korea
3. Teams tied on points after the group stage had to contest play-off matches; Switzerland and West Germany beat Italy and Turkey respectively and advanced to the knockout stages.
4. Two hat-tricks at the same World Cup
5. It was the only team to win a World Cup without playing a game against an opponent from any other continent, as Turkey, despite being geographically mostly in Asia, was invited through Europe.
6. Adolf 'Adi' Dassler, the founder of Adidas; he fitted longer, screw-in spikes to the West German players' boots, giving them added grip and extra stability on the muddy pitch.
7. Both the Asian qualifiers were played here for the 1954 World Cup – it was the last time the Asian Football Confederation

did not conduct World Cup qualification matches for the continent's FIFA member associations.

8. Zurich; the FIFA headquarters are based here.
9. Spain
10. He picked up a slip of paper with Turkey's name on it to decide the qualifier for the World Cup, after Turkey and Spain had played three games without a clear winner – they split points after the initial qualifiers and then drew the play-off.
11. Waldyr Pereira, famously known as Didi
12. Bill Shankly
13. Calcutta (now Kolkata)
14. Giampiero Boniperti
15. Alf Ramsey (coach of the 1966 winning team)

Solution to Connect

KOCSIS	WAGNER	HÜGI	PROBST	*1954 World Cup hat-trick scorers*
RAHN	WALTER	PUSKÁS	HIDEGKUTI	*Players in the 1954 World Cup final*
WANKDORF	HARDTURM	BERN	ZURICH	*Stadiums and host cities at the tournament*
ADIDAS	STUDS	RAIN	LEATHER	*Elements linked to the 1954 final conditions*

1958, SWEDEN

STORIES

Emergence of the Black Pearl

Pelé's emergence at the 1958 World Cup in Sweden was a seismic moment in sports history, an event where a 17-year-old not only announced himself to the world but altered the course of Brazilian football and provided the sport its first global superstar.

Pelé began the tournament on the bench due to a knee injury, missing the first two group matches. He made his debut in Brazil's third game against the USSR, providing an assist in a crucial 2–0 win that saw a dramatic shift in the team's attacking prowess with the inclusion of both him and the electric winger Garrincha.

It was in the knockout stages that he truly announced himself. In the quarter-final against Wales, he scored the only goal of the match, a precise finish that made him the youngest goalscorer in World Cup history at 17 years and 239 days. This was followed by a stunning hat-trick in the 5–2 semi-final victory over France. And then, in the final against hosts Sweden, after going down by a goal early, Brazil rallied, and Pelé sealed the win with two iconic goals in the 5–2 victory.

His first, where he controlled a cross on his chest, chipped the ball over a defender's head, and volleyed it home, remains one of the greatest World Cup goals ever scored. At the final whistle, the teenager was overcome with emotion, weeping on the shoulder of teammate Gilmar, as his promise to his father years earlier to win a World Cup for Brazil was fulfilled.

Pelé's impact transcended the pitch. He embodied *jogo bonito* the 'beautiful game' and its potential to lift an entire country. His rise from a disadvantaged background in Brazil to global fame offered hope and pride for millions.

The 1958 World Cup was the foundation of an unparalleled legacy, as he became the only player to win three World Cups, forever cementing his status as one of the greatest athletes of the century and as a defining figure in modern football history.

Just Fontai-stic!

Records are meant to be broken, yet some achievements feel surreal, almost unreachable for generations to come. Just Fontaine's astonishing tally of 13 goals at the 1958 World Cup belongs firmly in that rare category. More than a statistical marvel, his feat represents a moment when a goalscorer's instinct and artistry with the ball converged in a way that has never been emulated.

The Frenchman was the archetype of a natural goalscorer. Smooth, powerfully built and two-footed, he possessed remarkable calm inside the penalty area. Like the greatest finishers, he seemed to arrive at the ball before defenders realized danger existed. His physique, combined with extraordinary spatial awareness, made him lethal where it mattered most.

His journey to global immortality was far from straightforward. Born in Marrakech, Morocco, to a Spanish mother, Fontaine's path mirrored that of several great French players whose roots lay beyond mainland France. After beginning his career in Casablanca, he moved to Nice and then to Reims, where he was tasked with the daunting role of replacing the departing Raymond Kopa. Rather than letting that burden overwhelm him, Fontaine flourished, and by the time the World Cup arrived, he was at his peak, brimming with confidence after a prolific domestic season.

An injury to a teammate thrust Fonatine into the starting XI and he seized the opportunity with both hands. He scored in every match France played, six in total, beginning with a hat-trick against Paraguay and ending with four goals in the third-place play-off against West Germany.

Central to his success was his partnership with Kopa, whose vision and passing fed Fontaine a steady supply of chances. Their understanding was intuitive, almost effortless, and it dismantled defenses unprepared for such harmony. Against Northern Ireland, Fontaine's second goal was a masterclass in anticipation. Even in defeat, particularly against a brilliant Brazilian side, his quality shone through with a goal widely regarded as one of the finest ever seen on the World Cup stage.

What makes Fontaine's record even more remarkable were the conditions under which it was achieved. He played with borrowed boots, in an era without substitutions, on heavier pitches, with less protective refereeing and rudimentary support systems. There was no Golden Boot ceremony – only an air rifle as a token prize.

His career was unfortunately cut short by injury when he was just 28, yet he retired with an extraordinary scoring record that still defies belief.

Konspiration 58

This isn't a World Cup story, but it is interesting nevertheless! *Konspiration 58* (*Conspiracy 58*) was a Swedish documentary released more than four decades after the 1958 World Cup that presented a satirical conspiracy theory claiming the entire tournament never actually took place.

Produced by the Swedish public broadcaster Sveriges Television (SVT), the film was presented as a serious investigation into a fictional movement claiming the tournament was staged. The mockumentary proposed that the entire event was faked in the United States as a Cold War experiment orchestrated by the CIA, FIFA and television networks to test the power of televised propaganda. Led by director

Johan Löfstedt, the film's creators used various pieces of 'evidence' to support this absurd claim, such as analysing grainy footage to point out an alleged Los Angeles skyline in the background of a stadium or the supposedly incorrect angle of shadows for the Swedish summer.

When it first aired, the audience was not informed that it was a mockumentary, leading to widespread public confusion and numerous phone calls from viewers who were either convinced or angered by the claims.

While the film used the real events, scores and players of the 1958 World Cup, including Pelé's legendary performance, as its raw material, its primary purpose was not to insult the Brazilian win. Instead, it was a clever critique of media manipulation, the power of television and the willingness of people to believe in even the most outlandish conspiracy theories, when presented alongside widely accepted historical facts.

The film's effectiveness lay in its ability to convincingly blur the line between reality and fiction, using the cherished memory of Sweden's greatest sporting event as the perfect canvas for its social commentary.

The Fall of the Mighty Magyars

The Hungarian Revolution of 1956 sounded the death knell for Hungary's legendary 'Golden Team', aka the Mighty Magyars, a side that had revolutionized football tactics and gone 50 matches with only one loss between 1950 and 1956. The political turmoil led to the mass defection of key players, fundamentally weakening the national side and resulting in a disappointing performance at the 1958 World Cup in Sweden.

The core of the Hungarian national team played for the club side Budapest Honvéd. In October 1956, Honvéd was in Spain for a European Cup match against Athletic Bilbao when the anti-Soviet revolution erupted in Budapest. As Soviet tanks crushed the uprising, the players made the momentous decision not to return to Hungary, effectively choosing exile.

This mass defection was the single largest 'brawn drain' of athletes during the Cold War. The biggest stars, including Ferenc Puskás, Sándor Kocsis and Zoltán Czibor, all of whom were vital to the team's success, never played for the national team again.

The national team that travelled to the 1958 World Cup in Sweden two years later was a shadow of its former self. Only a few remnants of the original Golden Team remained, such as goalkeeper Gyula Grosics, defender József Bozsik, and forward Nándor Hidegkuti. The squad was primarily composed of younger, less experienced players who were expected to fill the immense void left by the defectors.

This new, weakened team struggled to make an impact. They were eliminated in the group stage after a play-off match. In their group, they drew 1–1 with Wales, lost 2–1 to the host nation Sweden and won 4–0 against Mexico. This left them level on points with Wales, necessitating a play-off match, which they lost 2–1, sealing their early exit from the tournament.

The 1956 revolution marked the abrupt end of an era of Hungarian football dominance and the beginning of a long period of decline, one from which the national team has never fully recovered. The Mighty Magyars were history, a victim of geopolitical conflict that dispersed one of the greatest teams never to win the World Cup.

Meticulously Planning a Maiden World Cup

Brazil's triumph at the 1958 World Cup was the result of a paradigm shift in their approach to the tournament. Haunted by the traumatic 'Maracanazo' defeat in the 1950 final and a disappointing exit in 1954, the Brazilian Football Confederation (CBF) planned a campaign that was meticulous and left little to chance.

They implemented a revolutionary plan devised by a multi-disciplinary commission. This group focused on every aspect of the team's welfare and performance. The national squad was surrounded by an unprecedented 22-person entourage including a technical supervisor, a doctor, a dentist, a psychologist, a physiotherapist, a trainer and a scout.

One of the most innovative aspects of Brazil's preparation was the use of science and psychology. The team doctor, Hilton Gosling, worked with a dentist to ensure all players had healthy teeth, believing that infections could affect athletic performance. The psychologist, João Carvalhaes, conducted tests on the players to assess their suitability for the pressures of international competition.

The team prepared for months at a training camp in the mountains near São Paulo to simulate the cooler European climate. Coach Vicente Feola, a man manager with a keen eye for talent, fostered a strong team spirit and introduced the revolutionary '4–2–4 formation' to the Brazilians that optimized Brazil's attacking flair while maintaining defensive solidity. He also had the foresight to manage the expectations and physical condition of his squad, resting key players like Pelé and Garrincha in the initial group games to unleash them fresh for the knockout stages.

They even arrived in Europe early, allowing ample time for acclimatization to Swedish conditions, a factor that had historically hindered South American teams when playing in Europe. They chose to base themselves in a quiet, isolated town in southern Sweden, away from the intense media scrutiny and the distractions of urban life.

This training cycle, a stark contrast to the more relaxed approaches of other nations, created an environment in which extraordinary talent could thrive and provided the foundation for the first team to win a World Cup outside its own continent.

QUIZ

Questions

Kick-Off

1. For the 1958 tournament, an Asian–African qualifying group was set up? Which team received walkovers from all three of their opponents, but then lost an intercontinental play-off to Wales and couldn't make it to the tournament?

2. What event, now a much-anticipated pre-World Cup tradition, was hosted on 8 February 1958 in Solna and hosted by TV show host, Otto Lennart Hyland, and journalist, Sven Jerring?
3. Seeding of teams for this tournament was geographical rather than based on team strength. Four groups were thus set up, containing one western European team, one eastern European team, one from the Americas, and one from which other grouping?
4. Which two countries played out the first-ever goalless draw in World Cup history in 1958? They have since played against each other in three more editions of the tournament with the same team emerging victorious each time.
5. In their semi-final against Brazil, with less than 40 minutes played and the score tied 1–1, which French player broke his leg in a clash with Vavá, thus reducing his team to ten men for the rest of the game? (Substitutions were not allowed at the time). Brazil dominated the rest of the match, with a Pelé hat-trick sealing a 5–2 victory.

Extra-Time

6. In this edition, if Pelé became the youngest player to play in, score in and win a World Cup final, which Swedish midfielder set the record as the oldest player to score in a World Cup Final at 35 years and 264 days?
7. Which stadium, built for the tournament, almost collapsed during a Bruce Springsteen concert on 8 June 1985, as thousands of people in the audience moved and swayed? Because the stadium was built on clay, it couldn't support such commotion – citing the same reason, David Bowie's Glass Spider Tour in 1987 was also relocated out of this famed venue.
8. Which future coach, who managed his country at three FIFA World Cups (1986, 1990, 1994) – leading them to the quarter-finals in Mexico 1986 (losing to Argentina) and the semi-finals in Italy 1990 (losing to West Germany on penalties), their best finish in 24 years – made his debut as a player in this tournament?

9. Which West German player, who later became the first to feature in 20 World Cup matches, the first to score in four World Cups, and the first to net at least two goals in each of the four World Cups, scored to put his country ahead in their opening game against Argentina as they set out to defend their title?
10. With a draw against Wales, which country scored their first point/achieved their first positive result, ending a run of eight straight defeats across its previous three appearances – and a ninth loss in its opening group match against Sweden? No other team has lost nine consecutive games in World Cup history.

Shoot-Out

11. What geographical feat did Brazil achieve at this tournament, which remained elusive to other teams till as recently as 2010? They repeated it in 1994, 1970 and 2002.
12. The architect of one of Hungarian football's greatest wins – a 6–3 drubbing of England in Wembley in 1953 – which talismanic striker was perhaps last of the golden generation of the Mighty Magyars to play in this edition? He had scored a hat-trick in that fixture and, despite being well past his prime and the upheaval of the Hungarian Revolution of 1956, turned up for his team in 1958.
13. Jernvallen Stadium in Sandviken hosted two games at this tournament – first Hungary vs Wales, then Hungary vs Mexico. What geographical distinction did it achieve, one that has yet to be surpassed in FIFA World Cup history?
14. In November 1957, FIFA launched a competition that received 102 entries. Submissions were mandated to be free of any marks or letters and accompanied by an envelope carrying the producer's name. At the office of the Swedish Football Federation at the Råsunda Stadium in Solna, Stockholm, a lawyer, – *Notarius Publicus*, or Public Notary, Mr Bengt Steuch – registered the entries and assigned them numbers from 1 to 102. In February 1958, a winner was picked (serial number 55,

with the original entry still preserved in that stadium). What was this competition meant to decide?

15. In an unusual move for the time, Idrætsparken Stadium was being considered as a possible venue for this edition. Why was it eventually discarded, thus preventing this tournament from becoming the first to achieve a distinction that is now held by the 2002 edition?

Word Search

The final and the third-place play-off from this edition remain among the highest-scoring games in FIFA World Cup history. Search this puzzle for the names of goalscorers from these games.

Note: Diacritics such as accents or tildes have been omitted.

U	N	R	J	J	C	P	A	F	G	P	I	E	I	S	D	I	P
Z	L	Z	Z	X	A	Y	A	T	P	W	L	T	J	O	V	X	J
O	N	K	S	W	D	J	S	X	A	C	I	H	I	K	A	L	F
A	A	W	K	A	Y	Z	P	K	U	G	E	Z	U	X	V	P	O
O	E	Q	K	H	F	I	Y	R	H	J	D	P	V	G	A	K	N
Z	A	G	A	L	L	O	V	R	H	E	H	D	E	F	R	N	T
Q	R	K	Z	W	O	Z	U	A	G	D	O	E	O	L	G	X	A
L	K	P	G	H	F	L	X	H	U	Z	L	U	R	U	E	V	I
I	O	E	F	L	Y	T	Q	N	G	B	M	B	O	D	I	V	N
H	P	W	C	I	E	S	L	A	R	C	Z	Y	K	V	L	S	E
Y	A	E	N	Y	A	W	H	D	S	C	H	A	F	E	R	O	N
A	O	N	V	J	H	A	S	I	M	O	N	S	S	O	N	H	E

Find the following words in the puzzle.
Words are hidden →, ↓, and ↘.

CIESLARCZYK
SIMONSSON
LIEDHOLM
FONTAINE
ZAGALLO
SCHAFER
DOUIS
PELE
VAVA
KOPA
RAHN

ANSWER KEY

Answers to Questions

1. Israel
2. The official draw
3. Great Britain (the only time all four constituent nations – England, Northern Ireland, Scotland and Wales – qualified for the World Cup)
4. Brazil and England
5. Robert Jonquet
6. Niels Liedholm
7. Ullevi in Gothenburg
8. Bobby Robson
9. Uwe Seeler
10. Mexico
11. Winning a World Cup in a continent that was not theirs. (Spain in 2010, Germany in 2014 and Argentina in 2022 have since emulated this.)
12. Nándor Hidegkuti
13. It is the northernmost venue to have hosted FIFA World Cup matches.
14. The official ball for the 1958 World Cup – Top-Star (VM-bollen 1958)
15. Idrætsparken, located in Copenhagen, had been planned as the venue for Denmark's group-stage matches. When Denmark failed to qualify, the idea was discarded. And thus two countries did not host this world cup. (The first such instance happened in 2002, when South Korea and Japan hosted the tournament.)

Solution to Word Search

```
. . . . . . . . . . . . . . . . . .
. . . . . . . . . . . L . . . V . .
. . . . . . . . . . . I . . . A . F
. . . . . . . . . . . E . . . V . O
. . . . . . . . . . . D P . . A . N
Z A G A L L O . R . . H D E . . . T
. . . . . . . . A . . O . O L . . A
. K . . . . . . H . . L . . U E . I
. O . . . . . . N . . M . . . I . N
. P . C I E S L A R C Z Y K . . S E
. A . . . . . . . S C H A F E R . .
. . . . . . . S I M O N S S O N . .
```

Word directions and start points are formatted: (Direction, X, Y)

CIESLARCZYK (E,4,10)
SIMONSSON (E,8,12)
LIEDHOLM (S,12,2)
FONTAINE (S,18,3)
ZAGALLO (E,1,6)
SCHAFER (E,10,11)
DOUIS (SE,13,6)
PELE (SE,13,5)
VAVA (S,16,2)
KOPA (S,2,8)
RAHN (S,9,6)

1962, CHILE

STORIES

Down but Not Out

Chile's recovery in order to host the 1962 FIFA World Cup stands as a testament to the nation's remarkable resilience and determination in the face of an unparalleled natural disaster. In May 1960, two years before the tournament, the country was struck by the Valdivia earthquake, the most powerful ever recorded (measuring 9.5 on the Richter scale), which caused catastrophic damage to infrastructure and left millions homeless. Despite widespread doubts and international pressure to move the competition, Chile pressed ahead, turning the monumental challenge into a symbol of national recovery.

The earthquake and subsequent tsunamis devastated large portions of the country, rendering four of the eight planned host cities (Talca, Concepción, Talcahuano and Valdivia) unusable. With the national infrastructure in ruins, many assumed hosting was impossible. However, the president of the Chilean Football Federation and head of the organizing committee, Carlos Dittborn, made an impassioned and famous plea to the FIFA Congress: 'Because we have nothing, we want to do everything (*Porque nada tenemos, lo haremos todo*).' This powerful sentiment, coupled with a diplomatic and detailed presentation, secured the hosting rights over a favoured Argentina.

With minimal government funding available for the World Cup due to the focus on broader national reconstruction, the organizing committee, aided by international donations and technical assistance from FIFA, embarked on a frantic rebuilding effort.

Tragically, Dittborn, the driving force behind the recovery, died just a month before the World Cup began. The stadium in Arica was named the Estadio Carlos Dittborn in his honour.

The tournament itself commenced on schedule, running from 30 May to 17 June, and was an organizational success that uplifted the spirits of a recovering nation.

So Good, That They Didn't Need Pelé

Pelé arrived at the 1962 FIFA World Cup in Chile at the peak of his young career, a reigning champion who had captured the world's imagination with his brilliance as a 17-year-old in Sweden four years prior. The stage was set for the 21-year-old phenomenon to dominate the tournament and cement his status as the undisputed king of football. Fate, however, intervened with a cruel injury, transforming his World Cup story from one of individual glory for Pelé to a powerful narrative about Brazil's team resilience and the rise of another legend, Garrincha.

Brazil began their title defence in confident fashion against Mexico on 30 May 1962. Pelé was exceptional, assisting one goal and scoring another with a typical moment of magic, beating two defenders before finding the net, in a comfortable 2–0 victory. The performance hinted at the spectacular tournament many expected from him.

The second group stage match against Czechoslovakia on 2 June, however, brought disaster. Early in the game, Pelé attempted a powerful, long-range shot. In doing so, he strained or tore a muscle in his left thigh. In an era before substitutions were permitted, a hobbled Pelé had to stay on the field, effectively a passenger on the left wing, for the remainder of the goalless draw. The injury was severe, immediately ruling him out for the rest of the competition. His World Cup was over as soon as it began.

The news was a huge blow to both the team and fans worldwide, who had hoped to see the sport's brightest star illuminate the Chilean grounds. Many pundits predicted Brazil's title defence would crumble without their talisman.

Pelé's early exit paved the way for his teammates to step into the spotlight. Amarildo filled the void at forward with aplomb, scoring a crucial goal in the final. More significantly, the irrepressible, bow-legged winger Garrincha took over as Brazil's driving force. With Pelé sidelined, Garrincha delivered a series of dazzling, near-unmarkable performances in the knockout stages, inspiring Brazil to the final.

In the final, once again against Czechoslovakia, Brazil triumphed 3–1. While Pelé could only watch from the sidelines, his absence ultimately highlighted the depth of talent within that exceptional Brazilian squad.

Battle of Santiago

The 'Battle of Santiago', an infamous Group 2 clash between the host nation Chile and Italy at the tournament, is widely regarded as the most violent match in FIFA World Cup history. Beyond the final 2–0 scoreline in favour of Chile, the game is remembered for its lack of sportsmanship, multiple police interventions, and its enduring legacy on rules of football.

The animosity between the two nations was ignited by reports from Italian journalists Antonio Ghirelli and Corrado Pizzinelli, who described Santiago as a 'backwater dump' characterized by poverty, alcoholism and crime. These remarks were deeply offensive to a nation still recovering from the catastrophic 1960 Valdivia earthquake. Chilean newspapers retaliated by labelling the Italians as 'fascists' and 'mafiosi'. By the time the players stepped onto the pitch at the Estádio Nacional, the atmosphere resembled a battlefield rather than a sporting event.

English referee Ken Aston, who later described his role as an 'umpire in military manoeuvres', struggled to maintain control from the start. The first foul occurred just 12 seconds in, and the first player was sent off in the eighth minute. Giorgio Ferrini was dismissed for a foul on Honorino Landa but refused to leave the field; armed police eventually had to drag him off. Later, Chile's Leonel Sánchez, the son of a professional boxer, broke Italian captain Humberto Maschio's nose with a left hook. Surprisingly, Sánchez was not sent off, but the Italian he had struck, Mario David, was dismissed minutes later for a retaliatory high kick to Sánchez's head. Scuffles, spitting and frequent punches were reported throughout the 90 minutes, and police were forced to enter the field four separate times to restore order, as players prioritized fighting over playing football.

As news travelled across the globe, the reaction was one of pure shock. BBC commentator David Coleman famously introduced the highlights by calling the game 'the most stupid, appalling, disgusting and disgraceful exhibition of football, possibly in the history of the game.'

The positive legacy of the game was the modernization of football refereeing though. Ken Aston's frustration with the language barriers and the difficulty of communicating dismissals during the match (and a similar incident later in 1966) led him to invent yellow and red cards. Inspired by the clarity of traffic lights, he proposed the system to FIFA, and it was successfully introduced at the 1970 World Cup in Mexico.

The Little Bird Who Soared Highest

Garrincha's performance at the 1962 FIFA World Cup in Chile is perhaps the greatest individual display in the tournament's history. While Brazil arrived as favourites, the world expecting another masterclass from Pelé, a cruel injury to the star forward in the second match changed the narrative. In Pelé's absence, the spotlight shifted to the bow-legged, irrepressible winger from the dusty fields of Pau Grande. Manuel Francisco dos Santos, known universally by his childhood nickname Garrincha – the name of a small Brazilian bird – did not just fill the void; he soared, almost single-handedly carrying Brazil to their second consecutive World Cup title.

At 28 years old, Garrincha was already a beloved figure for his dazzling dribbling skills and child-like joy for the game. When Pelé was sidelined with a thigh injury during the goalless draw against Czechoslovakia, the burden of creativity and goalscoring fell squarely on Garrincha's shoulders.

Garrincha's brilliance was unleashed in the knockout stages. In the crucial quarter-final against England, he was unplayable. He terrorized the English defence with his unpredictable swerves and searing pace. He scored two goals: a powerful header from a corner kick and a stunning, curling shot from outside the box. Brazil won 3–1, and the world began to realize that the Seleção, Brazil's national team, had a new talisman.

His semi-final performance against the host nation, Chile, was even more dominant. In a hostile atmosphere, Garrincha single-handedly dismantled the home side's defence, scoring two more goals in a 4–2 victory. His first was a low, precise shot, and the second a spectacular header, demonstrating his aerial ability despite his short stature. His performance was so impactful that even the home crowd applauded him. This match, however, was marred by a moment of indiscretion; Garrincha was sent off in the final minutes for kicking a Chilean player after persistent fouling, meaning he would miss the final.

Fortunately for Brazil, a combination of diplomatic lobbying by Brazilian officials and the referee's lenient match report allowed the suspension to be overturned. Garrincha was free to play in the final against Czechoslovakia.

In the final, with Pelé watching from the sidelines, Garrincha continued to mesmerize. Despite having a fever, he was the primary creative force, running the opposition defence ragged. Brazil won the final 3–1, securing their title defence and cementing Garrincha as the undisputed star of the 1962 World Cup. He was awarded the best player of the tournament and was also the joint top scorer with four goals.

Greaves' Grief

One of the most bizarre and humorous anecdotes from the tumultuous 1962 World Cup in Chile involves the English striker Jimmy Greaves and a stray dog. The incident occurred during England's quarter-final against Brazil.

In the first half of the match, as Brazil held a 3–1 lead, a small dog wandered onto the pitch. The dog proceeded to run around the field, evading all attempts by players to catch it, much to the amusement of the Viña del Mar crowd.

Greaves decided to try his luck. He got down on all fours and whistled, attempting to coax the dog towards him. His approach worked, and the dog trotted over. However, as Greaves reached out to grab it, the dog urinated all over his famous white England kit.

The stadium erupted in laughter, and even the players, including the Brazilians, could not suppress their amusement at the absurdity of the whole situation.

The incident became a memorable piece of World Cup folklore, a moment of light-hearted absurdity in a tournament otherwise known for its rough play and an intense atmosphere. Greaves himself often recounted the story with humour in later years, forever linking his name with that unexpected canine encounter on football's grandest stage.

QUIZ

Questions

Kick-Off

1. Which 'union' between two countries from separate continents, that was soon dissolved, had been invited to play in the qualifiers for this tournament, which began in late 1960? Heralded at the time as a significant moment in fostering unity, the team never

played a game though. Following Sudan's withdrawal, the group was eventually declared void by FIFA.

2. What feat achieved by Attilio Demaría and Luis Monti in 1934 was emulated by Ferenc Puskás, José Santamaría and José Altafini at this edition of the World Cup?
3. Name the president of the organizing committee who lobbied to get the World Cup to Chile and then oversaw preparations as his country overcame one of the most powerful earthquakes ever recorded in order to stage the tournament. He tragically passed away a month before the start of the event.
4. Who was named as Pelé's replacement after the great exited the tournament after playing just once, in Brazil's opening match against Czechoslovakia? With big boots to fill, the 22-year-old striker made an instant impact, scoring 2 goals against Spain and also netting the equaliser in the final, repaying the faith shown in him by manager Aymoré Moreira.
5. The 1962 World Cup remains the only edition of the tournament to have as many as six joint top scorers. If Chilean Leonel Sánchez, Hungarian Flórián Albert, Soviet Valentin Ivanov and Yugoslavian Dražan Jerkoviž were four who shared the honour, which two talismanic Brazilians completed this list?

Extra-Time

6. Two managers achieved the distinction of having coached their respective national teams at a fourth World Cup in 1962. While Walter Winterbottom had done so across successive editions, which German coach had been in charge at the last World Cup before the Second World War and then again from 1954 to 1962?
7. Which African team, who scripted history at the 2022 World Cup, topped their group in the qualifiers for the 1962 edition but were eliminated by Spain in an intercontinental play-off? They eventually made their debut at the tournament in 1970.

8. What World Cup first was achieved by Marcos Coll of Colombia, when he beat the legendary goalkeeper Lev Yashin in a 4–4 draw against the Soviet Union at this edition? While such incidents are not uncommon in world football, this remains the only instance of its kind at the World Cup.
9. One of the groups in this tournament saw two teams tied for the second spot with an equal number of points. For the first time in World Cup history, goal average was used to segregate teams, allowing England to qualify for the quarter-finals at the expense of which iconic rival?
10. Which iconic right-back, playing his third successive World Cup, noticed that the Czechoslovak goalkeeper Viliam Schrojf was somewhat off his line and lofted a long, massive, high-arcing ball into the goalmouth to aid Brazil's last goal in the final?

Shoot-Out

11. Which star player, sent off during the semi-final against host nation Chile after reacting to repeated fouls, had his ban for the final overturned following heavy lobbying by team officials as well as his country's prime minister?
12. Who officiated the infamous 'Battle of Santiago', the ill-tempered group match between hosts Chile and Italy that descended into violence and persistent rough play from both sides? Coincidentally, he never refereed another game at the World Cup but went on to be a part of FIFA's referees' committee and oversaw match officials for the 1966, 1970 and 1974 World Cups.
13. This edition of the World Cup was the last not to be televised live in Europe. Name the first series of satellites that revolutionized global communication, launched in mid-1962, ensuring that future editions of the tournament could be broadcast live. (Hint: The satellites' name has a World Cup connection.)
14. The hosts surprisingly reached the semi-finals, prompting FIFA to switch their match against defending champions Brazil to the National Stadium in Santiago in anticipation of a massive

crowd. Which venue was originally scheduled to host that semi-final, one which eventually ended up hosting the other semi-final between Czechoslovakia and Yugoslavia?

15. What World Cup record did Václav Mašek set in a match against Mexico at this edition, a record that stood for forty years before being broken by a Turkish player at the 2002 FIFA World Cup?

Word Search

A big factor for Brazil defending its title in 1962 was the continuity of the squad from the previous edition in 1958. Search through this puzzle to name the players who were part of both World Cup–winning campaigns.

Note: Diacritics such as accents or tildes have been omitted.

C	A	S	T	I	L	H	O	K	D	Y	U	G	A	J	P	Z	E
Z	J	I	O	S	G	A	R	R	I	N	C	H	A	K	I	B	U
I	M	Y	U	U	Y	T	J	J	W	M	Z	V	A	V	A	G	Z
T	H	L	H	E	M	X	O	Z	O	Z	I	M	O	V	T	U	S
O	M	G	I	L	M	A	R	S	D	Z	H	D	I	D	I	B	L
X	W	S	R	A	A	K	Y	E	T	I	I	W	V	P	I	M	Z
M	A	R	I	O	Z	A	G	A	L	L	O	K	O	X	E	V	I
Q	P	M	M	A	U	R	O	R	A	M	O	S	Q	S	F	L	H
T	E	I	Y	D	J	A	L	M	A	S	A	N	T	O	S	H	E
H	P	F	W	N	I	L	T	O	N	S	A	N	T	O	S	X	J
A	E	G	S	M	I	I	G	U	J	F	N	N	Q	I	U	P	T
J	O	J	B	K	Q	J	G	X	V	D	D	Z	L	A	S	I	R

Find the following words in the puzzle.
Words are hidden →, ↓, and ↘.

MARIO ZAGALLO	CASTILHO	VAVA
NILTON SANTOS	GILMAR	ZITO
DJALMA SANTOS	ZOZIMO	PEPE
MAURO RAMOS	PELE	
GARRINCHA	DIDI	

ANSWER KEY

Answers to Questions

1. United Arab Republic (a short-lived political union between Egypt and Syria)
2. Representing a second country at the tournament. (Puskás had played for Hungary in 1954, Santamaría for Uruguay in 1954, and they both played for Spain in 1962. While Altafini, who had played for Brazil in 1958, represented Italy in 1962.)
3. Carlos Dittborn
4. Amarildo
5. Garrincha and Vavá
6. Sepp Herberger
7. Morocco, who in 2022 became the first African team to reach the semi-final of the FIFA World Cup
8. Olimpico, or the Olympic goal – scored directly from a corner kick
9. Argentina (Both teams finished the group stage with 3 points, but England had a goal average of +1, while Argentina's was –1.)
10. Djalma Santos
11. Garrincha
12. Ken Aston (He also introduced yellow and red cards to football.)
13. Telstar (It was also the name of the first official Adidas match ball, used at the 1970 World Cup.)
14. Sausalito Stadium, Viña del Mar
15. Fastest goal (Václav Mašek scored after just 16 seconds.)

Solution to Word Search

```
C A S T I L H O . . . . . . . . . .
Z . . . . G A R R I N C H A . . . .
I . . . . . . . . . . . V A V A . .
T . . . . . . . Z O Z I M O . . . .
O . G I L M A R . . . . D I D I . .
. . . . . . . . . . . . . . P . . .
M A R I O Z A G A L L O . . . E . .
. P . M A U R O R A M O S . . . L .
. E . . D J A L M A S A N T O S . E
. P . . N I L T O N S A N T O S . .
. E . . . . . . . . . . . . . . . .
. . . . . . . . . . . . . . . . . .
```

Word directions and start points are formatted: (Direction, X, Y)

MARIO ZAGALLO (S,17,1)
NILTON SANTOS (S,9,1)
DJALMA SANTOS (E,1,1)
MAURO RAMOS (S,8,2)
GARRINCHA (S,7,2)
CASTILHO (S,12,2)
GILMAR (S,5,6)
ZOZIMO (S,2,3)
PELE (S,6,5)
DIDI (S,16,4)
VAVA (E,10,10)
ZITO (E,13,8)
PEPE (S,11,3)

1966, ENGLAND

STORIES

Lost and Found

The story of the 1966 World Cup trophy being stolen against the backdrop of one of England's greatest sporting moments is fascinating to say the least.

In March 1966, the Jules Rimet Trophy, the coveted prize of international football, was on public display at a stamp exhibition in Methodist Central Hall, Westminster, London. Valued at less than the rare stamp collections surrounding it, its actual security was surprisingly minimal. On 20 March, a daring thief exploited this oversight, breaking through a rear door and a flimsy display case while a church service was underway there. The priceless symbol of global football vanished, sending shockwaves through the Football Association (the FA) and the British public just months before the World Cup was due to begin in England.

The situation quickly turned worse. The FA chairman, Joe Mears, soon received a ransom demand for £15,000. Scotland Yard launched a major investigation, setting up a sting operation where an undercover detective posed as Mears' assistant. The meeting with the middleman, Edward Betchley (who went by the name 'Jackson'), in Battersea Park was tense. Betchley, an East London docker, became spooked by surveillance and was arrested, though he maintained he was merely a go-between for a mysterious figure known only as 'The Pole'. Betchley was convicted, but the actual thief and the trophy's location remained elusive. The crisis deepened, fueling fears that the World Cup itself might be cursed or compromised.

The nation's anxiety was finally put to rest a week later, on Sunday, 27 March. In the quiet suburban streets of Beulah Hill, South London, David Corbett was out with his black-and-white collie, Pickles, when the dog began to eagerly sniff at a parcel wrapped in an old newspaper and tied with string, hidden under a hedge. Corbett initially thought it might be a bomb, but eventually gave in to his curiosity and unwrapped the package to discover the gleaming gold trophy. He immediately took his astonishing find to the local police station.

The discovery turned Pickles into an instant celebrity. He became a national hero overnight, gracing television screens, starring in a film, and attending the World Cup victory banquet later that summer with his owner after England lifted the very same recovered trophy.

Phantom Goal

In the 101st minute of the 1966 World Cup final, with the score deadlocked at 2–2, England's Geoff Hurst unleashed a powerful shot that would spark a debate lasting decades and eventually reshape the laws of the game.

The drama unfolded when Hurst received a cross from Alan Ball, swiveled, and struck a rising shot from close range. The ball hammered against the underside of the crossbar, rocketed down onto the turf, and then bounced back out into the field of play. While England striker Roger Hunt immediately wheeled away in celebration, the West German defenders and goalkeeper Hans Tilkowski were adamant that the ball had not crossed the line.

Caught in the middle was Swiss referee Gottfried Dienst. Unsure of the call, he consulted his linesman, Tofiq Bahramov. Bahramov, an Azerbaijani official from the Soviet Union, confidently signalled that it was a goal. This decision gave England a 3–2 lead and paved the way for their eventual 4–2 victory, securing their first and only World Cup title.

For nearly 60 years, the 'Wembley Tor' (Wembley Goal), as it is known in Germany, has been subjected to endless scrutiny. German players at the time claimed to have seen chalk dust fly as the ball hit the line, suggesting it never fully crossed. In contrast, Bahramov later maintained in his memoirs that he believed the ball had actually hit the back of the net, not the crossbar, making its point of impact on the ground irrelevant in his mind.

Modern scientific analysis has added fuel to the fire. Various studies using computer simulations and film analysis have largely concluded that the ball did not fully cross the line, falling short by approximately 6–18 centimetres. Conversely, some sports broadcasts have used advanced digital rendering to argue that the decision was actually correct.

Perhaps we will never know for sure!

North Koreans Thrive Despite Political Tensions

North Korea's participation in the 1966 World Cup in England is one of the competition's most extraordinary and inspiring stories. Arriving as relative unknowns and massive underdogs, the team, nicknamed 'Chollima' after a mythical winged horse, defied political barriers and sporting expectations to capture the hearts of the English public and make history as the first Asian team ever to reach the quarter-finals.

The journey began with a politically fraught qualification process. Due to boycotts by African nations protesting the lack of guaranteed spots and discrimination, North Korea only had to defeat Australia in a two-legged play-off, which they did convincingly with a 9–2 aggregate score. Their arrival in the United Kingdom presented a diplomatic challenge, as the British government did not officially recognize North Korea at the time. However, FIFA insisted on their participation.

The team was based in Middlesbrough for their group stage matches in Group 4, which included formidable opponents: the Soviet Union, Chile, and the two-time world champions, Italy. The locals quickly grew fond of the disciplined and good-humoured North

Korean players. Their campaign started with a predictable 3–0 loss to the USSR, followed by a 1–1 draw against Chile, with Pak Seung-zin scoring their first-ever World Cup goal. To advance, they needed a victory in their final match against the heavily favored Italians.

In one of the greatest upsets in World Cup history, a goal from the celebrated Corporal Pak Doo-ik in the 42nd minute secured a shocking 1–0 victory for North Korea. This resulted in Italy's elimination from the tournament and sent North Korea unexpectedly into the quarter-finals, a first for any Asian nation. The people of Middlesbrough embraced their adopted team, with an estimated 3,000 fans travelling to Liverpool's Goodison Park to cheer them on in the quarter-final against Portugal.

The fairy tale almost continued in the quarter-final. North Korea stormed to a stunning 3–0 lead within just 25 minutes thanks to goals from Pak Seung-zin, Li Dong-woon and Yang Seung-kook. However, Portugal's legendary striker Eusébio single-handedly turned the tide, scoring four goals in an incredible comeback to seal a 5–3 victory for the Portuguese.

Despite the heartbreaking loss, the North Korean team returned home as national heroes, earning the world's respect and leaving a lasting legacy as one of the World Cup's most memorable underdogs. Their improbable run was later chronicled in the 2001 documentary film *The Game of Their Lives*, directed by Daniel Gordon, ensuring the memory of the 'People's Republic of Middlesbrough' endures in football history.

Greyhound Racing over World Cup Football

In a bizarre footnote to the history of the World Cup, one group stage match at this edition was forced to move from the iconic Wembley Stadium, not due to weather or safety concerns, but because the venue's owners refused to cancel a regularly scheduled greyhound racing event. This curious incident highlighted the immense popularity and commercial power of dog racing in mid-twentieth century Britain, even in the face of the world's most prestigious football tournament.

The match in question was the Group 1 clash between Uruguay and France, initially slated for Wembley. However, the game was scheduled for a Friday, a traditional night for greyhound racing at the stadium. The stadium's owners, prioritizing their established commercial commitments and regular income from the dog track, declined all requests to postpone or cancel the race meeting for the football match.

This refusal by the stadium's owners led to the match being hastily relocated to the White City Stadium in West London. White City, originally built for the 1908 Olympics, was also a major greyhound racing venue but was available on the scheduled date. The switch resulted in a less-than-ideal setup for a World Cup match as the stadium was primarily designed for athletics and dog racing. As a result, the football pitch was set far back from the stands, offering a poor viewing experience for the 45,662 fans who attended the game.

The decision drew quiet criticism at the time and was an awkward moment for the local tournament organizers and FIFA. It seemed inconceivable that the national stadium of the host nation would prioritize a domestic animal race over a major international football fixture. The event stands in stark contrast to the modern era of global sports, where multi-billion dollar contracts and immense broadcast demands would make such a scheduling conflict unthinkable.

Weekly Off!

The 1966 World Cup remains the only FIFA tournament in history where no matches were played on Sundays. This scheduling anomaly was not a logistical decision but a reflection of the prevailing religious laws in Britain at the time, specifically the Sunday Observance Act, which significantly restricted commercial and public activities on the Sabbath.

In the mid-1960s, a strong current of Sabbatarianism still influenced British life and legislation. Laws designed to ensure

Sunday remained a day of rest and worship meant that organizing large-scale professional sporting events was legally complex, if not impossible, in many jurisdictions. Local councils and stadium owners were bound by these restrictions, and the tournament organizers had to meticulously plan the entire World Cup schedule to accommodate this cultural and legal framework.

Consequently, all 32 matches of the tournament were held on weekdays or Saturdays. The tournament began on a Monday, 11 July, and the final was deliberately scheduled for Saturday, 30 July, to avoid any conflict with the Sunday laws. This need to adhere strictly to the calendar was a logistical challenge, compressing the group stage and knockout rounds into a tighter timeframe and ensuring sufficient rest days were available without playing on Sundays.

The impact was evident throughout the competition's planning. When a group match between Uruguay and France was originally planned for Wembley Stadium on a Friday, it had to be moved to White City Stadium because Wembley's owners prioritized a lucrative, regularly scheduled greyhound racing event over the football match, as the race fit within their permitted activities on that day. Such constraints added further challenge to what was a scheduling nigthmare.

The rigid observance of Sunday as a day without professional football was a cultural relic that began to fade in the following years.

QUIZ

Questions

Kick-Off

1. Fifteen countries from which continent withdrew from the qualifying rounds of the 1966 World Cup since they were not guaranteed a spot in the finals? FIFA had ruled that they would need to play inter-continental play-offs, as in previous editions, and this didn't go down well with them.

2. What first in FIFA World Cup history is credited to Reg Hoye, a children's book illustrator?
3. While the iconic Wembley hosted all but one of the games that took place in London, which stadium, built for the 1908 Olympics, hosted the Uruguay vs France fixture? Also, what was the reason Wembley wasn't allowed to host that game?
4. Famous withdrawals, including that of an iconic sprinter from the 1924 Olympics, had occurred for this reason, but never before had a World Cup been made to schedule its games in accordance with such a restriction. What scheduling-related issue is being discussed here?
5. Due to which country's qualification did the British government instruct the organizers to play the national anthems of the teams only at the opening match and the final? The diplomatic scrutiny surrounding this team's participation was immense, and the initial plan was to deny their players visas. Fearing backlash for dragging politics into sport, however, the UK government finally relented.

Extra-Time

6. Much like Garrincha in 1962, which then 20-year-old player, who had scored 4 goals and impressed with his link-up play, was due to miss the final because of bookings, but FIFA decided to ignore his second yellow card as a case of mistaken identity, and he was allowed to play? (He had received two yellow cards against Argentina and the USSR in the semi-final.)
7. In one of the weirder moments in the tournament, what was Argentine captain Antonio Rattín's persistent request, one that delayed the game as he was being sent off by German referee Rudolf Kreitlein?
8. What was the name of the legendary BBC commentator who uttered these famous words after Geoff Hurst's third goal at the

end of extra time: 'Some people are on the pitch. They think it's all over... It is now!'?

9. The English Football Association indulged in an duplicative endeavour ahead of the final – one that yielded over £2,50,000 at a 1997 auction. What did they do?
10. Cristiano Ronaldo has now scored in five consecutive World Cups, amassing a total of 8 goals. He is, however, still second on the list of Portugal's all-time World Cup goalscorers. Which star from 1966, who played in just six games at what was his only World Cup, leads that table with 9 goals?

Shoot-Out

11. On Sunday, 20 March 1966, what happened at the 'Sport with Stamps' Stanley Gibbons Stampex rare stamp exhibition at Methodist Central Hall in Westminster?
12. Pelé and Garrincha had scored to lead Brazil to a routine win in their opener against Bulgaria in this edition. Which country, however, handed them their first World Cup loss since 1954 in a group game at Goodison Park? Brazil subsequently lost their final group game against Portugal and were eliminated at the group stage.
13. Despite the unanimous boycott by his continent, which referee was chosen by FIFA to officiate the group-stage game between North Korea and Chile? As a clue, he also refereed the much-talked-about and controversial Mexico vs El Salvador game at the 1970 FIFA World Cup.
14. When England were drawn in the same group as Azerbaijan in qualifying for the 2006 FIFA World Cup, a ceremony was held at the stadium in Baku to honour which figure who had become iconic at the 1966 tournament? A statue of him was also unveiled, as he became the first referee to have a stadium named after him.
15. A 2013 report by historians from Humboldt University found a 1966 letter from the chairman of the FIFA medical committee

referencing 'very fine traces' of the banned stimulant ephedrine in three unidentified players during the 1966 World Cup. The discovery was part of a broader study alleging widespread, systematic, and state-funded doping across sports for decades. Which country's players were the subject of these findings?

Anagrams

Unscramble the following to name five of the iconic venues used for the games at the 1966 World Cup in England.

1. BLIGHLOORUSH
2. OGODPONIARKS
3. AFFORDDORTL
4. EARMARKSEPOY
5. IETWITCHY

ANSWER KEY

Answers to Questions

1. Africa
2. He was the creator/designer of World Cup Willie, the mascot of the 1966 World Cup. (This was the first ever FIFA World Cup mascot.)
3. White City Stadium; the owner of Wembley refused to cancel regularly scheduled greyhound race that was taking place on the same day, and therefore the match had to be moved to White City Stadium.
4. No games on Sundays. (Eric Liddell had refused to run in the 100-metre heats at the 1924 Olympics because they were scheduled on a Sunday.)
5. North Korea
6. Franz Beckenbauer

7. He wanted a translator, as he wished to explain his actions to the referee after being sent off.
8. Kenneth Wolstenholme
9. They made a replica of the Jules Rimet Trophy for security contingencies and post-final celebrations. FIFA bought it in an auction in 1997 for the said amount.
10. Eusebio
11. The Jules Rimet Trophy, which was exhibited there, got stolen.
12. Hungary
13. Ali Hussein Kandil from Egypt
14. Tofiq Bahramov, the linesman who allowed Geoff Hurst's second goal in the final
15. West Germany

Solutions to Anagrams

1. Hillsborough (Stadium)
2. Goodison Park
3. Old Trafford
4. Ayresome Park
5. White City (Stadium)

1970, MEXICO

STORIES

Brazil Gets to Keep the Trophy... Or Do They?

The 1970 World Cup in Mexico marked a historic moment as it was the first time a nation could claim permanent ownership of the coveted Jules Rimet Trophy. The rule, established by Jules Rimet himself, the former FIFA president, stipulated that the trophy would become the permanent property of the team that achieved a third tournament victory at least in theory!

Brazil, having previously won in 1958 and 1962, entered the tournament with a golden generation of players and a perfect winning record throughout both their qualifying matches and the final tournament itself. In the final at the Estadio Azteca in Mexico City, they faced Italy, who had won the World Cup twice before (in 1934 and 1938). Brazil's superior attacking play shone through in the second half, with goals from Pelé, Gérson, Jairzinho and Carlos Alberto sealing a decisive 4–1 victory.

Following the triumph, the Jules Rimet Trophy was presented to the Brazilian Football Confederation (CBF) headquartered in Rio de Janeiro, where it was displayed in a cabinet with a bulletproof glass front. However, the trophy's story took a sad turn when it was stolen in December 1983 by thieves who managed to pry open the wooden rear of the cabinet. The original trophy has never been recovered. A replica was later commissioned and presented to the CBF in 1984.

The permanent awarding of the trophy to Brazil prompted FIFA to commission a new design for the next tournament. The current FIFA World Cup Trophy was introduced for the 1974 World Cup. Under the new rules, no nation can keep the current trophy permanently, regardless of how many times they win; the original remains in FIFA's possession, and Brazil is the only team in history allowed to keep the World Cup!

Der Kaiser Plays Through Game of Century with a Sling

On 17 June 1970, West Germany faced Italy in the semi-final at the Estadio Azteca in Mexico City, a match that would later be dubbed the 'Game of the Century'. The game was a fierce battle and remained tied at 1–1 at the end of normal time. Early in the game, Beckenbauer was fouled just outside the Italian penalty area, an incident some Germans believed should have been a penalty. In his desire to show the referee the foul, he fell heavily, resulting in a dislocated right shoulder and possibly a broken collarbone.

The critical situation for West Germany was that they had already used both of their permitted substitutions, as only two were allowed as a rule at the time. This meant that if Beckenbauer left the field, his team would have to play the remaining extra time with only 10 men. Displaying extraordinary courage and determination, Beckenbauer refused to leave the game. An improvised sling was fashioned to strap his injured arm to his body, and he played on in obvious pain for the rest of the match.

Despite his limited mobility, 'Der Kaiser' (The Emperor), as he was nicknamed, continued to organize his team from defence. The match became an end-to-end thriller during extra time, with five goals scored in the added period – a World Cup record. Ultimately, Italy secured a dramatic 4–3 victory, but Beckenbauer's warrior-like spirit became an enduring symbol of German fighting spirit and an iconic moment in World Cup history.

Captain Seals the World Cup with a Wonder Goal

Carlos Alberto's iconic goal in the 1970 World Cup final, Brazil's fourth in a 4–1 victory over Italy, is widely regarded as one of the greatest goals in football history. It was the perfect culmination of a near-perfect tournament.

A result of a breathtaking team move involving all but two of Brazil's outfield players, showcasing vision even when victory was all but sealed, the move began deep in the Brazilian half, near the penalty area, when Tostão retrieved a loose ball.

After a few initial passes in defence, defensive midfielder Clodoaldo received the ball and proceeded to dribble past four Italian players in his own half, elegantly evading their challenges with a shimmy and a series of changes of pace. Clodoaldo then passed to Rivellino on the left wing. He swept a precise 40-yard pass down the line to Jairzinho, who ran at the defence before cutting inside and poking the ball to Pelé on the edge of the penalty area. Pelé, with his back to the goal and the Italian defender Tarcisio Burgnich blocking his path, paused and, without looking, casually rolled the ball into the path of the onrushing Carlos Alberto.

Brazil's captain, who had made a surging run from his right-back position into the attack, met the ball just inside the box. He didn't break stride, unleashing a powerful, first-time shot across the goal and into the bottom-left corner of the net past the Italian goalkeeper Enrico Albertosi.

The goal, scored just four minutes from the end of the match on 21 June 1970, was the perfect final flourish to a dominant display and sealed Brazil's third World Cup title, earning them the right to keep the Jules Rimet Trophy permanently. Its legacy still endures, and as Carlos Alberto himself recollected later, 'I realize how beautiful and how important that goal was because everybody is still talking about it... My pride is in finishing the goal of all our team, for the football of Brazil…'

Peru's Iconic Kit

Peru's kit at the 1970 World Cup, with its distinctive red diagonal sash across a plain white shirt, is widely considered one of the most beautiful and iconic football jerseys of all time. The simple yet striking design became a symbol of the team and a badge of belief for them as they reached the quarter-finals in what many regard as a golden era for football in the South American nation.

The core design of the kit – a white shirt exquisitely dissected by a bold red diagonal sash running from the left shoulder to the right hip – was first adopted at the 1936 Berlin Olympics, reportedly inspired by school matches where sashes helped distinguish teams. In the 1970 iteration, the sash was particularly wide and prominent, paired with a stylish collared V-neck, that added to its legend.

The colour combination – with the white representing peace and purity, while the red depicting the courage and the blood spilled by the nation's heroes – made for an enduring design, known as *La Blanquirroja* (the white-and-red), and marked Peru's first appearance in the tournament after four decades as they eliminated Argentina in the qualifiers.

Led by legends such as Teófilo Cubillas, Héctor Chumpitaz and Hugo Sotil, the team's performance on the field was perfectly matched by the elegance of their kit, and onlookers couldn't stop lauding it, with many calling it the 'beautiful game's most beautiful shirt'.

The team's golden era, which included a Copa América win in 1975 and another World Cup qualification in 1978, further added to the jersey's legend, with the 1978 version of the kit even topping a 2010 ESPN list of the Best World Cup jerseys of all time.

Jairzinho's Feat

It was at this edition that Jairzinho the extraordinary feat of scoring in every single match Brazil played on their path to lifting the Jules Rimet Trophy.

Nicknamed Furacão (Hurricane) due to his explosive pace and power, Jairzinho played as a right-winger in the 1970 tournament, and his game was defined by blistering runs down the flank and clinical finishing. He formed a devastating attacking quartet with Pelé, Tostão and Rivellino, a combination that tormented opposing defences throughout the competition.

His consistency was unmatched. He scored two in Brazil's opening match against Czechoslovakia, followed by another brace against England in a famous encounter that also featured Pelé's iconic header, which Gordon Banks' saved. He continued this scoring streak in every subsequent game: against Romania, in the quarter-final against Peru, and in the semi-final against Uruguay.

Then in the final against Italy on 21 June 1970, Jairzinho ensured his place in footballing immortality by scoring Brazil's third goal in a resounding 4–1 victory. It was a typical Jairzinho goal, finishing off a flowing team move after initiating the move himself.

This goal was his seventh of the tournament.

This unique achievement of scoring in every match of a World Cup edition has never been replicated, and although Gerd Müller of West Germany won the Golden Boot with ten goals, the Brazilian icon's seven goals across six matches remain a distinct achievement from the tournament.

QUIZ

Questions

Kick-Off

1. Which stadium that hosted the opening game of the 1970 edition would also be doing the same in the 2026 tournament? While its original name paid tribute to an ethnic group that dates back to the thirteenth century, naming rights were recently bought by which company, thus lending it a new identity?
2. Which English player was detained in Bogotá, Colombia, during a stopover en route to the 1970 World Cup after being accused of stealing a bracelet, sparking a diplomatic incident

and a period of house arrest before ultimately being released due to lack of evidence?

3. At this edition, which Soviet player made history by becoming the first substitute to appear in a FIFA World Cup match, coming on for Viktor Serebryanikov at half-time in their game against Mexico on 31 May 1970, marking the debut of the tournament's new substitution rule?
4. In the qualifiers for the 1970 World Cup, which team – quarter-finalists at the previous edition – were North Korea drawn to face in the second round of the Asian/Oceania play-offs? Citing political reasons, North Korea refused to play the matches and was disqualified from the competition. Their opponents subsequently advanced and qualified for what remains their only World Cup appearance.
5. In 1970, who became the first person to win the World Cup as both a manager (1970) and as a player (1958 and 1962)? In addition, he won the 1994 World Cup as assistant manager.

Extra-Time

6. Which goalkeeper produced what is now dubbed the 'save of the century' during a 1970 World Cup group-stage match between England and Brazil in Guadalajara, Mexico? He miraculously denied a powerful downward header from Pelé with a last-second acrobatic dive, tipping the ball over the crossbar with his fingertips.
7. Forming a partnership with FIFA in 1970, which Italian company published its first World Cup sticker album for this edition, initiating a global craze for collecting and trading stickers? In 2017, a complete 1970 World Cup sticker album signed by Pelé sold for a record £10,450.
8. The 1970 FIFA World Cup semi-final between Italy and West Germany was truly iconic. After Roberto Boninsegna had scored in the eighth minute for Italy, Karl-Heinz Schnellinger scored his only international goal in injury time to level the

match and force extra time. Five more goals were scored by both teams in extra time, with Italy advancing to the final. What is this match iconically referred to as?

9. Although they withdrew from some previous editions, 1970 remains the only instance in which the illustrated team unsuccessfully attempted to qualify for the World Cup? Which team was it? They finished last in their group – behind Peru and Bolivia – in the CONMEBOL (South American Football Confederation) qualifiers for the 1970 tournament held in Mexico.
10. What did FIFA commission a replica of – made by Eastman Kodak using 1.8 kilograms of gold – that was presented to Brazilian military president João Figueiredo in 1984?

Shoot-Out

11. Which 21-year old burst onto the scene at the 1970 World Cup in Mexico, scoring five goals to help his team reach their first-ever quarter-final and earning the FIFA Young Player Award? So impressive was he that Pelé dubbed him his successor after his memorable performance against Brazil, where he scored his fifth goal, cementing his status as a rising star.
12. In the 1970 semi-finals, Brazil faced Uruguay for the first time since the decisive final-round match of the 1950 World Cup. During the 1970 encounter, Pelé produced one of his most famous plays. After receiving a through ball from Tostão, the Brazilian great reached it before Uruguay's goalkeeper, cleverly letting it run past without touching it, causing it to roll to the keeper's left, while he moved to the right. Pelé then went around the goalkeeper and took a shot while turning towards the goal. But he turned in excess as he shot, and the ball drifted just wide of the far post. Despite not resulting in a goal, it remains one of the most iconic moments of the tournament. What was the name of the Uruguayan goalkeeper who was at the receiving end of this mastery?
13. What was the name of the stadium in León used at this World Cup? It hosted seven matches, including all of Group 4's fixtures

and a quarter-final. Although located in Mexico, its name is perhaps more synonymous with the home ground of a club from another continent.

14. Which striker scored 10 goals at this edition to win the Golden Boot and was nicknamed 'Der Bomber' because of his devastating goal-scoring ability, said to 'explode' opposition defences with sudden, lethal strikes, much like a bomber plane destroying its targets?
15. What anomaly was observed in matches such as Germany vs Peru and atleast the first half of the Italy vs Germany semi-final? In retrospect, it was quite ironic given this was the first World Cup to be televised live in colour.

Connect

Group the 16 words into four groups of four. Each group shares a common connection. Each word belongs to one group only.

PELÉ	AZTECA	MOORE	YELLOW
ITALY	TROPHY	URUGUAY	DEYNA
SUBSTITUTE	ARDILES	ENGLAND	TELEVISION
LEÓN	TOLUCA	PERU	GUADALAJARA

ANSWER KEY

Answers to Questions

1. Estadio Azteca (Azteca Stadium) in Mexico City. It has been renamed Estadio Banorte after Banorte, a financial institution, bought naming rights.
2. Bobby Moore
3. Anatoliy Puzach
4. Israel

5. Mario Zagallo
6. Gordon Banks
7. Panini
8. Game of the Century
9. Argentina
10. The Jules Rimet Trophy (It was awarded to Brazil for becoming the first team to win it thrice.)
11. Teófilo Cubillas of Peru
12. Ladislao Mazurkiewicz
13. Estadio León, commonly known as Nou Camp (Camp Nou in Barcelona, Spain, is the famous home stadium of FC Barcelona.)
14. Gerd Müller
15. Some matches were played with balls other than the official Telstar. Only 20 official balls were provided for the tournament and, thus, at times, organizers supplied brown leather balls or plain white ones instead. On colour television, these stood out noticeably.

Solution to Connect

PELÉ	MOORE (Bobby)	ARDILES (Osvaldo)	DEYNA (Kazimierz)	*Players from 1970 WC who were part of the film* Escape to Victory
AZTECA	GUADALAJARA	LEÓN	TOLUCA	*Host cities/ venues*
ENGLAND	PERU	URUGUAY	ITALY	*Opponents Brazil Faced in 1970*
YELLOW (cards introduced)	SUBSTITUTE (substitutions allowed)	TELEVISION (first global color broadcast)	TROPHY (Brazil kept the trophy permanently)	*1970 World Cup firsts and milestones*

1974, WEST GERMANY

STORIES

A Tumultuous Debut for Zaire

Zaire (now the Democratic Republic of the Congo) made history as the first Sub-Saharan African nation to qualify for the World Cup finals at this edition, a pioneering achievement not just for them but for the entire continent, which had until then not been allotted an automatic spot in the tournament.

The central African country arrived in West Germany as the reigning African Cup of Nations champions, a talented squad brimming with players from the nation's dominant clubs, such as TP Mazembe and Vita Club. However, having been drawn into a formidable Group 2 alongside Scotland, Yugoslavia and the reigning champions Brazil, the Zairians faced an uphill battle.

Their opening match against Scotland was a respectable 0–2 loss, a performance that suggested the team could compete. However, the campaign quickly went downhill. A devastating 0–9 defeat to Yugoslavia followed, a result that stands as one of the heaviest losses in World Cup history. This match exposed many deep-rooted issues beyond the football pitch, too. Political interference from dictator Mobutu Sese Seko's regime was rampant, with reports of players' bonuses being withheld by corrupt officials. The mental and emotional strain on the squad was immense.

The final group match against Brazil is perhaps the most remembered, though not for the football. Facing the world champions, with the looming threat of severe repercussions back home if they lost by too large a margin, Zaire employed desperate tactics.

The defining image of their tournament occurred when a Brazilian free-kick was about to be taken. Zaire defender Mwepu Ilunga sprinted from the defensive wall and booted the ball upfield. Referee Nicolae Rainea booked him, an act that bewildered commentators and spectators alike. Decades later, Ilunga explained it was a calculated act of time-wasting and subtle protest, a plea for help and a way to avoid the wrath of Mobutu. Zaire ultimately lost the match 0–3, concluding their World Cup journey with zero points, zero goals scored, but not without leaving their mark on the global stage.

East Trumps West

Drawn in Group 1, East Germany's only appearance at the FIFA World Cup was defined by their final first-round match against West Germany in Hamburg on 22 June 1974. Before this historic match, both teams had already secured their place in the second round, having played Australia and Chile. East Germany had defeated Australia 2–0 and drawn with Chile 1–1, while West Germany had beaten both teams. The match therefore decided which team would top the group.

In a tense game, East German striker Jürgen Sparwasser scored the only goal in the 77th minute, famously evading two defenders before shooting the ball past West German goalkeeper Sepp Maier. The victory made Sparwasser a national hero in East Germany and is often referred to simply as 'The Sparwasser Goal'. The match was laden with political symbolism, viewed by the East German communist government as a class struggle victory.

Ironically though, the victory may have hindered East Germany's progress in the tournament. By finishing first in Group 1, they advanced to a tougher second-round group (Group A) with powerhouses like the Netherlands, Brazil and Argentina. They ended up losing to the first two and drawing against Argentina, thus finishing third in their second-round group and being eliminated from the tournament.

Meanwhile, the defeat against East Germany prompted a realignment within the West German team, which went on to win all their subsequent matches in the easier Group B and ultimately defeated the Netherlands in the final to become world champions.

Total Football

The 1974 FIFA World Cup served as the ultimate unveiling of 'Total Football', a revolutionary tactical system orchestrated by Dutch coach Rinus Michels and implemented by the genius of Johan Cruyff.

The Netherlands, a team that had not qualified for the World Cup in 36 years, captured the imagination of the world with a fluid style of play that made players and supporters sit up and take notice.

Central to Total Football was the principle of constant movement and positional interchangeability, where any outfield player could seamlessly take over the role of any other player. This created a 'controlled chaos' that was unpredictable for opponents, as defenders might suddenly join the attack and forwards would drop deep to defend or act as a playmaker. This system demanded that skill be coupled with game awareness, and Cruyff, with his vision, intelligence and exceptional ability on the ball, was the perfect orchestrator of this system. He functioned as a false nine, roaming across the pitch, directing teammates' movements and creating space and chances for others.

Throughout the tournament, the Dutch team, often referred to as Oranje (orange), delivered scintillating performances, including a dominant 4–0 victory over Argentina and a 2–0 win against Brazil in the second group stage, with Cruyff scoring in each of those two crucial matches. It was during the match against Sweden that Cruyff produced one of the tournament's most iconic moments: the 'Cruyff Turn', an audacious feint and pivot that left defender Jan Olsson bewildered and became a signature skill taught to players for generations.

The Netherlands entered the final against host West Germany as favourites, but were ultimately defeated 2–1, largely due to the West German team's effective man-marking, specifically Berti Vogts' job on Cruyff. Despite falling short, they are celebrated as one of the greatest teams never to win the World Cup and are widely credited with having influenced modern football, inspiring coaches and teams around the world.

Haiti on the Right and Wrong Side of History

Haiti's qualification was a landmark moment for the Caribbean nation's football history, marking their first and only appearance in the World Cup until their recent qualification for 2026.

Drawn into a challenging group with pre-tournament favorites Italy, Poland and Argentina, the Haitian team, primarily composed of amateur players, faced a daunting task that was further complicated by the brutal dictatorship of Jean-Claude Duvalier back home. They expectedly lost all three matches, but their campaign is remembered for a moment of glory in their opening match against Italy.

Gli Azzurri (The Blues; Italy) had not conceded a goal in over 1,142 minutes across 12 international matches, a world record for goalkeeper Dino Zoff. Early in the second half, Haiti's star striker Emmanuel Sanon broke clear and scored, shocking the football world and ending Zoff's remarkable streak. Though Italy went on to win the match 3–1, the goal became a legendary moment in Haitian sports history, bringing global recognition and pride for the nation. Sanon scored Haiti's other goal in their final match, a 4–1 loss to Argentina.

Off the pitch, however, the team faced several challenges. Following the Italy match, Haitian defender Ernst Jean-Joseph failed a drug test and was subsequently beaten as per reports by members of the Tonton Macoutes, Duvalier's feared secret police or the vice-president of the Haitian FA, major Acedius St Louis, and forcibly flown back to Haiti. This act of violence, coupled with concerns about the dictator's influence and the players' well-being, deeply affected the team. The players were reportedly terrified, which contributed to their heavy 0–7 defeat to Poland in their second game. Despite these immense pressures, the Haitian players remained resilient, earning the admiration and support of German fans.

Ultimately, while their results placed them 15th out of 16 teams, Haiti's campaign went beyond the scorelines. It was every bit as dramatic as those of other more successful teams and one that is still revered by the tiny Caribbean nation.

A Sixth Continent Finally Makes It to the World Cup

The 1974 World Cup in West Germany finally saw representation from Oceania, making it the sixth continent to play in the World Cup. The qualifying path for Australia, which finally succeeded in making it to the tournament, was arduous – a team comprised mostly of part-time players, navigating through the Asia–Oceania qualifying zone, which involved almost a dozen matches across various countries. Coached by the Yugoslav-born Rale Rasic, their campaign involved extensive travel as well.

Key moments in that journey included topping a preliminary Asia–Oceania group featuring New Zealand, Indonesia and Iraq. They then defeated Iran in a two-legged play-off, holding on for an aggregate victory in front of a hostile crowd of 1,20,000 in Tehran. The final hurdle was a two-match series against South Korea, which resulted in two draws (0–0 and 2–2). A decisive third match on neutral ground in Hong Kong saw Jimmy Mackay score a memorable long-range goal to secure a historic 1–0 victory and Australia's first-ever World Cup berth.

At the tournament itself, they were drawn into a formidable Group 1 alongside the host nation and eventual champions West Germany, their political counterparts East Germany and Chile. The consensus among the world press gave the amateur Socceroos little hope against such elite, professional opposition, and they eventually ended up losing to the first two.

Against Chile, however, in a hard-fought match played in driving rain, the Socceroos secured their first and only point of the tournament with a scoreless draw. This result remained their only point at the World Cup until the team qualified again over three decades later in 2006.

QUIZ

Questions

Kick-Off

1. In an otherwise immaculate campaign, champions West Germany suffered only one loss (in their final group stage fixture). Which debutant, who never played another edition, beat them?
2. Which country, making their first appearance at the World Cup since 1938, demonstrated a style of play pioneered by the top team in their domestic league, in which specialised positions were virtually abolished for the outfield players, and individual players became defenders, midfielders, or strikers as the situation required?
3. Following a military overthrow of President Salvador Allende and his Popular Unity coalition government, which country refused to travel to Chile for the second leg of their

intercontinental play-off and thus missed out on qualification for this World Cup?

4. Emmanuel Sanon scored against Italy in their opening game, ending goalkeeper Dino Zoff's run of most minutes played without conceding a goal in international football. Which country was he representing, one that hasn't played in a World Cup since?
5. In their game against Brazil, which Zaire defender darted out of the defending wall before a free kick and kicked the ball away as hard as he could? Initially perceived to be a mistake, he later clarified that he was protesting against his government, which had refused to pay them match fees, and thus wished to get sent off.

Extra-Time

6. Red cards were formally introduced in World Cup play four years before this, but no players were sent off in that tournament. That changed in this edition though. Which South American player became the first player to be sent off with a red card in tournament history?
7. Just a minute into the final, Dutch skipper Johan Cruyff was brought down by Uli Hoeneß inside the penalty area, and they were awarded a penalty. Who converted from the spot, thus handing his team the lead before any West German player had even touched the ball?
8. Which Indian-born referee officiated Poland's 7–0 win over Haiti, thus becoming the first Asian ever to be appointed as the referee for a World Cup fixture? He edged Iranian Jafar Namdar, who made his tournament debut with the whistle three days later.
9. Designed by Silvio Gazzaniga, the manufacture of what involved skilled craftspeople at the company GDE in Milan (now Stabilimento Artistico Bertoni), manually chiselling brass with grinders and chisels, followed by mechanical brushing and polishing before electroplating?

10. What ignominious distinction does Haiti defender Ernst Jean-Joseph hold in World Cup history?

Shoot-Out

11. What record did Poland's Lesław Ćmikiewicz set at this edition? His feat, which wasn't possible before 1970, was eventually emulated by Brazil's Denilson in 1998, who currently holds the overall record.
12. Who did the hosts beat in the semi-final, which has since been dubbed the 'Frankfurt Water Fight' or the 'Water Battle of Frankfurt'? Played in torrential rain on a flooded pitch, their opponents, who were top scorers in the tournament till then, accused the hosts of tampering with the drainage, claiming that the water favoured the German team's more physical play over their faster, more skilful style.
13. What phrase is usually used to describe a classic football feint where a player fakes a pass or shot with their foot, then instantly pulls the ball back behind their standing leg, spinning 180 degrees to change direction and leave the defender wrong-footed? If it serves as a hint, it was first performed famously against Sweden's defender Jan Olsson at the 1974 World Cup, bamboozling him and introducing the move to the world.
14. A World Cup record set in this edition that is still unmatched is that of most players from one team scoring in the same game. Which team was this, who had seven different scorers in their record 9–0 win over tournament debutants Zaire?
15. Who received a 14-week ban from football, which made him ineligible for the World Cup for abusing a referee in a Bundesliga game just before the tournament, and thus unable to feature? His absence ensured that two sets of twins didn't feature in the edition – Rene and Willy van de Kerkhof did so, and his brother Helmut also played in the tournament.

Crossword

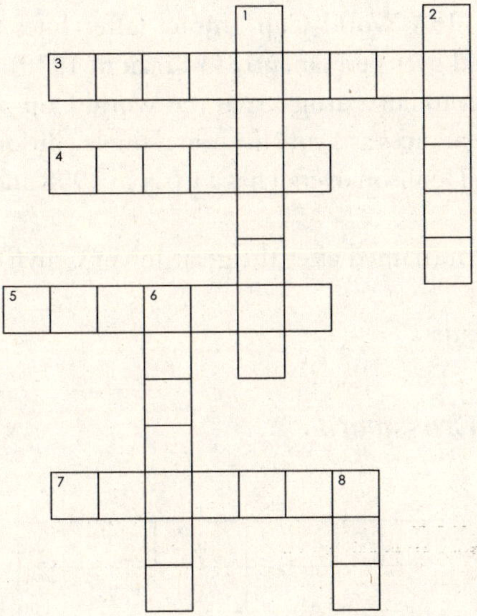

Across: →

3. First edition for a 6th continent
4. Only team to hold the Dutch
5. Northern-most venue
7. Suffix in official name of ball

Down: ↓

1. Golden Boot
2. Referee from Iran
6. State in which final took place
8. One of the mascots

ANSWER KEY

Answers to Questions

1. East Germany
2. Netherlands (Total Football)
3. USSR
4. Haiti (They qualified again for the 2026 edition, marking their second appearance at the tournament, 52 years after the first.)
5. Mwepu Ilunga
6. Carlos Caszely

7. Johan Neeskens
8. George Govindasamy Suppiah
9. The new FIFA World Cup Trophy (after Jules Rimet Trophy was handed over permanently to Brazil in 1970)
10. First player to fail a drug test at the World Cup
11. Most appearances as a substitute at a single edition of the World Cup (six); Denilson overall has 11 (six in 1998 and five in 2002)
12. Poland
13. Cruyff Turn (named after the great Johan Cruyff)
14. Yugoslavia
15. Erwin Kremers

Solution to Crossword

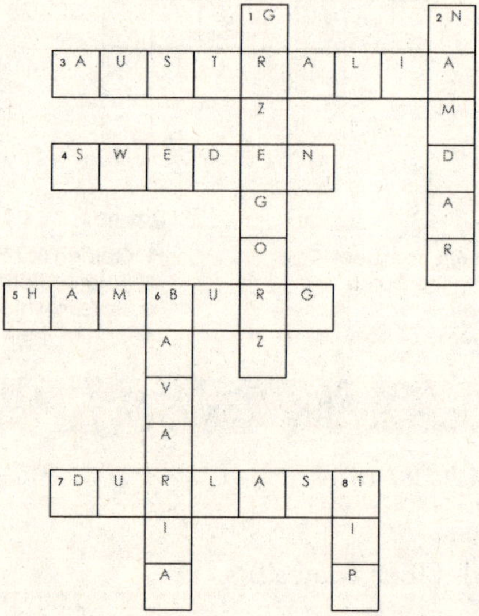

Across: →

3. First edition for a 6th continent
4. Only team to hold the Dutch
5. Northern-most venue
7. Suffix in official name of ball

Down: ↓

1. Golden Boot
2. Referee from Iran
6. State in which final took place
8. One of the mascots

1978, ARGENTINA

STORIES

A Military Diktat

Argentina's military regime, led by General Jorge Rafael Videla, which came to power after the 1976 coup, organized the 1978 FIFA World Cup like no other. Awarded hosting rights in 1966 under a democratic government, the tournament almost became a centrepiece for the junta's efforts to project stability and modernity, yet the shadow of unrest remained over the tournament.

The regime invested over $700 million, far in excess of initial budgets, to build three new stadiums (in Córdoba, Mar del Plata and Mendoza) and renovated others like River Plate's Estadio Monumental, which hosted the final. The regime's urban renewal programme displaced shantytown residents to construct roads, hotels and press centres. Labourers worked under military oversight and union bans.

To rebrand Argentina as peaceful, a million-dollar PR campaign was ordered as well, targeting Western media with sponsored tours and countering human rights reports. State media censored dissent, portraying unity, while the logo evoking former President Juan Perón's salute was retained despite objections due to commercialization and legal concerns. Videla greeted teams and dignitaries like Henry Kissinger, using the event to deflect 'anti-Argentine plots' amid global scrutiny.

During preparations, repression intensified: dissidents faced secret detention, with some prisoners said to be close enough to hear stadium roars while enduring torture. The regime paused overt violence near journalists' hotels pre-tournament but resumed covertly, shifting tactics in response to media presence. Mothers of the Plaza de Mayo, a group of disappeared victims' mothers, marched weekly, gaining foreign coverage despite arrests, like Swedish player Ralf Edström's brief detention.

From 1 to 25 June, across six venues, Argentina qualified from its group despite a loss to Italy, then advanced via a 0–0 draw with Brazil and a suspicious 6–0 win over Peru, needing four goals after Brazil's result, sparking match-fixing claims involving grain shipments or dissident exchanges. In the final, hosts beat the Netherlands 3–1 after extra time, with Mario Kempes scoring twice; Dutch protests over delays and injuries highlighted biases.

The victory bolstered the junta in the short term, but long-term allegations of 'sportswashing' have tainted the event's legacy ever since.

Miracle or Disgrace

Played on 21 June 1978, the 'Miracle of Córdoba' between Austria and the reigning champions West Germany has etched itself into the collective memory of both nations.

For Austria, it was pure, unadulterated triumph over a country that had annexed it during the Second World War. The term 'miracle' aptly describes the victory. Austria, a capable but rarely dominant footballing nation, had not beaten its powerful neighbours in 47 years. Going into the match, the stakes were low for the Austrians; they were already eliminated from the second-round group stage. West Germany, however, needed a win to keep their hopes of defending the trophy they had won in 1974 alive.

West Germany initially took the lead through Karl-Heinz Rummenigge. But the second half exploded with drama. A peculiar own goal by German defender Berti Vogts levelled the score, and then the legendary Austrian striker Hans Krankl put Austria ahead. The Germans equalized almost immediately, setting up a frantic final twenty minutes.

In the 88th minute, Krankl scored his second goal, securing a historic 3–2 victory. In Austria, the euphoria was immediate and total. The radio commentary by Edi Finger, whose voice cracked with emotion, screaming 'Tor, Tor, Tor!' became iconic. The win had no bearing on the final tournament standings but became a source of immense national pride.

The German perspective offers a stark contrast: an event they dubbed the 'Disgrace of Córdoba'. It marked the end of an era, serving as the final match for their long-serving and highly successful manager, Helmut Schön. The shock elimination of the defending champions was also considered humiliating and a difficult end to a campaign that had promised much.

No Maradona, No Problem

The decision by Argentine coach César Luis Menotti to drop the 17-year-old Diego Maradona from the final squad for the 1978 FIFA World Cup on home soil is one of the most talked-about omissions in football history. Despite being a rising star and already a full international, Maradona was left out because Menotti believed he was too young to handle the immense pressure of a home tournament. This was a crushing blow for the young prodigy.

Leading up to the 1978 World Cup, the teenage Maradona was a sensation for his club, Argentinos Juniors, scoring prolifically and enthralling crowds with his talent. He had already made his senior international debut at age 16, just four months after his professional debut. Fans and media alike expected him to be a key part of Argentina's campaign to win their first World Cup. However, the coach had other ideas. Facing pressure not just from the public but also the country's ruling military junta, Menotti made the pragmatic decision to go with more experienced, proven players. Menotti felt that Maradona, though talented, was not yet physically and emotionally mature enough to cope with the burden and scrutiny of playing in such a high-stakes, politically charged environment.

The news brought dejection for the youngster, who was reportedly found crying his eyes out under a tree at the training base when he learned of his omission. He later wrote in his autobiography that the snub was the 'biggest disappointment' of his life, and the resulting anger became fuel for him.

Menotti's decision was controversial at the time, but in hindsight, it is often viewed as a pragmatic move that ultimately served both the team and the player's long-term career. Argentina went on to win the 1978 World Cup without Maradona, with Mario Kempes emerging as the tournament's star player.

The prodigy, driven by the disappointment, got even better. A year later, in 1979, he captained Argentina to victory in the FIFA World Youth Championship in Japan, and was awarded the Golden Ball as the tournament's best player. This win confirmed his status as a world-class talent and set the stage for his World Cup debut in 1982.

A Goal Disallowed Controversially

In the final seconds of Brazil's opening game against Sweden on 3 June 1978, in Mar del Plata, Zico headed in a winner – or so he thought.

Just a minute before, with the match tied at 1–1 in injury time, Brazil won a corner kick. The Welsh referee, Clive Thomas, allowed the corner to be taken, but as the ball was in the air from Nelinho's kick, he blew the final whistle, ending the match. Just a fraction of a second later, Zico rose to head the ball into the net. The Brazilian players and fans erupted in celebration, only to be left stunned and furious as the referee signalled that the goal did not count because the game had already ended.

By the letter of the law, Thomas was technically correct; the game ends the moment the final whistle is blown, regardless of the ball's position. However, given the standard practice for referees to allow a play to conclude, his decision was widely criticized. Many argued that he should have let the corner kick sequence finish before ending the match, especially given the potential game-winning impact. The Swedish defenders themselves were seen to stop playing after hearing the whistle, which is why Zico had a free header.

The 1–1 draw proved to be a costly result for Brazil. They went on to draw their next group match against Spain and, although they went unbeaten in the second group phase, they finished behind hosts Argentina on goal difference, missing out on a place in the final.

Had Zico's goal counted, the extra point from that match would have likely seen Brazil top their first-round group ahead of Austria and given them a different route in the second round, potentially altering the entire outcome of the tournament.

The incident is often cited as a prime example of a referee making himself the centre of the story and a controversial interpretation of the rules. Clive Thomas, known for his strict adherence to the book, was a contentious figure and did not referee another match in that World Cup following the widespread criticism.

Black and White Goalposts

The white with a black stripe goalposts at the 1978 World Cup in Argentina had a multifaceted story: they were a blend of practical stadium tradition and, according to some accounts, a subtle, clandestine form of remembrance for those who 'disappeared' under the country's military dictatorship. While often assumed to be purely a design choice for visibility, particularly on black-and-white televisions, a deeper political meaning has also been suggested by some individuals involved at the time.

The practice of painting goalposts with various patterns, including black-and-white stripes, was not unique to the 1978 World Cup and was a common practice in certain regions and clubs prior to FIFA standardizing the goalpost colour to white. The organizing committee for the World Cup sourced ground staff from local clubs, who brought their own regional ideas for goalpost designs, which created uniformity issues across the different stadiums. FIFA's preference was for consistency, but the local traditions, including the use of 'L-supports' for nets and painted posts, influenced the final look of the pitches. The stripes were also thought to aid visibility for players and spectators, especially on older television sets.

Years later, a former groundsman named Ezequiel claimed the black bands served a secret, solemn purpose. He stated that ground staff, appalled by the human rights abuses of the military junta and the forced disappearances of thousands of citizens, wanted to protest but feared for their safety.

Unable to stage a public demonstration, they decided to paint the black bands on the goalposts as a public 'black armband' in memory of the victims, hidden in plain sight. They allegedly told the clueless generals it was merely a football tradition.

This powerful narrative has been disputed by some Argentine media and observers, who point out that black-and-white goalposts were common before 1978 and argue against a specific political motive in that instance. Regardless of the definitive truth behind the intent, the striped goalposts remain one of the defining visual memories of the 1978 World Cup, which was staged amid widespread repression and international scrutiny of Argentina's military government.

QUIZ

Questions

Kick-Off

1. Which Argentine politician's signature gesture of extending both hands above his head was the basis of the tournament's logo? The only President of the country to be elected thrice, his family's regime was cut short due to the military coup in 1976, and despite repeated efforts to let go of his shadow from the tournament, the logo stayed.

2. Usually reserved for goalkeepers, why was midfielder Norberto Alonso handed the number '1' T-shirt for Argentina at this World Cup? The same logic was applied in the next edition when another outfield player, Osvaldo Ardiles, wore the number '1'.
3. Defending runners-up the Netherlands received a shock defeat in their final group stage fixture against Scotland. Which legendary player and a future managerial great scored first for the Scots to level the game just before half-time?
4. Which continental opponent did Argentina need to beat by four goals in their last second-round match to reach the final? They won 6–0 amid widespread speculations of foul play.
5. Which was the only team not to lose a single game at this edition of the World Cup? Despite their unbeaten record, they didn't go on to win the tournament, eventually finishing third.

Extra-Time

6. Argentine officials filed a complaint before the final via captain Daniel Passarella by protesting which Dutch player's lightweight cast on his fractured wrist? The hosts demanded extra bandages, which postponed the start of play and was seen by many as a stalling tactic to settle the hostile crowd.
7. Inspired by a popular dance form from the region, what was the name of the official ball from this edition, one that used a new feature of having a thin synthetic material on the cover to make it more impermeable to rain? The design, although modified, lasted two decades and was used at World Cups till as late as the 1990s.
8. Asia and Oceania had been allotted a single spot at this edition. Which country overcame former attendees like South Korea and Australia to have an unbeaten qualifying campaign and make it to their first ever FIFA World Cup?
9. Which Dutch player scored four penalty kicks during the 1978 FIFA World Cup, converting all of them, matching Eusebio's

record for penalties taken and scored in a single edition, and has since been emulated by Lionel Messi?

10. Backed by the military government that had taken over the country, the new Argentine Football Association president Alfredo Cantilo signed, leading up to the tournament, a resolution that prohibited international transfers of most players from the country. Who was the only player from the winning squad of 1978 who was exempted from this?

Shoot-Out

11. Which venue, named after a former River Plate and Argentina player and manager, became the southernmost ever to host FIFA World Cup matches at this edition?
12. Daniel Passarella, who was 25 years and 1 month old, remains the youngest captain to lift the World Cup trophy. He had, however, only taken over the responsibility shortly before the tournament because of which first-choice skipper retired, citing personal reasons?
13. Which manager was in charge of his national team for the fourth straight World Cup, setting records for both coaching the most matches (25) and the most wins (16) at the tournament, and was also the first coach to win both a World Cup and a European Championship in the same cycle?
14. In Brazil's game against Sweden, which player had his late header from a corner kick disallowed by Welsh referee Clive Thomas, who blew the final whistle before contact with the ball was made? The score remained 1–1 and meant that the three-time champions didn't qualify first from their group.
15. In 1978, Argentina became the first team to win the World Cup while including a squad member who was not playing club football at the time. Who was the player who, despite a six-month absence from club football due to a contract dispute with Boca, became the youngest member of Menotti's squad?

The left-back went on to play every minute of every match in the tournament.

Anagrams

Unscramble the following to name five of the players who scored three or more goals at the 1978 FIFA World Cup.

Note: Diacritics such as accents or tildes have been omitted.

1. GMMERINGUE
2. BERKSRENNIN
3. EPISOMEKAMR
4. CUREID
5. DOUPOOLEQUELL

ANSWER KEY

Answers to Questions

1. Juan Domingo Perón
2. Argentina allotted jersey numbers in alphabetical order (of surnames).
3. Kenny Dalglish
4. Peru
5. Brazil
6. René van de Kerkhof
7. Tango
8. Iran
9. Rob Rensenbrink
10. Mario Kempes (He was playing for Valencia in Spain.)
11. José María Minella Stadium in Mar del Plata
12. Jorge Carrascosa
13. Helmut Schön
14. Zico
15. Alberto Tarantini

Solutions to Anagrams

1. Rummenigge
2. Rensenbrink
3. Mario Kempes
4. Dirceu
5. Leopoldo Luque

The ball proposed by Argentina for the Final

The ball proposed by Uruguay for the Final

The Estadio Centenario inaugurated for the first FIFA World Cup

The 1930 FIFA World Cup finals being held at Estadio Centenario

Jules Rimet

Gianpiero Combi and Ricardo Zamora, goalkeepers and captains for Italy and Spain respectively

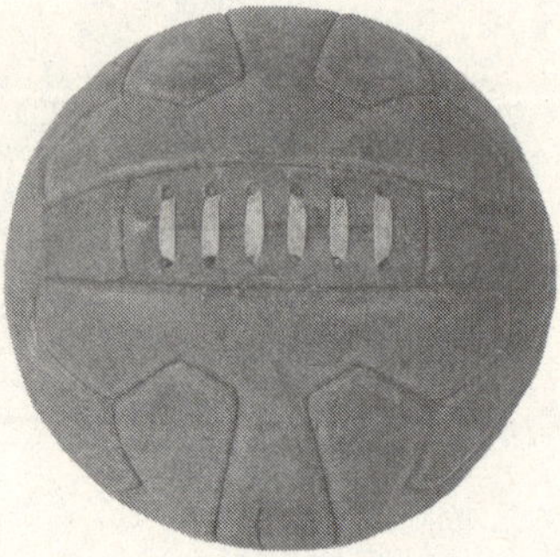

Federale 102: Official match ball of the 1934 FIFA World Cup

The Coppa Del Duce commissioned by Benito Mussolini

Matthias Sindelar: The Mozart of football

Italy celebrating their win

President Albert Lebrun of France presenting the trophy to Giuseppe Meazza

The World Cup final

Ernst Wilimowski: The first man to score four goals in a single World Cup game

Mo Heng Tan: Dutch East Indies goalkeeper

Gre-No-Li: The Swedish trio

Tragedy Superga: A sad and dark day for Italian football

Ghiggia with the Jules Rimet Trophy

The Italian team

Maracanã Stadium filled to capacity

The Swedish team

Ghiggia scores the winning goal in the World Cup final against Brazil

Grande Torino: Multiple-time champions of Italian football

Indian Team that went to play for the Olympic Games of 1952

Presentation of the Jules Rimet to West Germany's victorious captain, Fritz Walter

World Cup 1954 Final in Bern

The captains of the World Cup final, Walter and Puskás along with the referee

The Golden Generation of Hungarian football

Battle of Santiago: A tense affair between Chile and Italy in 1962

The Brazilian team before the 1958 World Cup final against Sweden

Pelé in the final

Brazil national team after winning the Cup

Carlos Dittborn (centre): Driving force behind Chile's successful bid to host the tournament

Estadio Carlos Dittborn: One of the four host stadiums

Brazil's Amarildo Tavares (at a league match)

The Italian team prior to the match against Israel

Challenge 4-Star: FIFA World Cup 1966 official match ball

A stuff toy of World Cup Willie, the official mascot 1966, displayed in a museum

A plaque honouring Pickles the dog

The Champions statue at Upton Park, London. It shows Bobby Moore, Geoff Hurst, Martin Peters and Ray Wilson holding up the only FIFA World Cup trophy won by England till date.

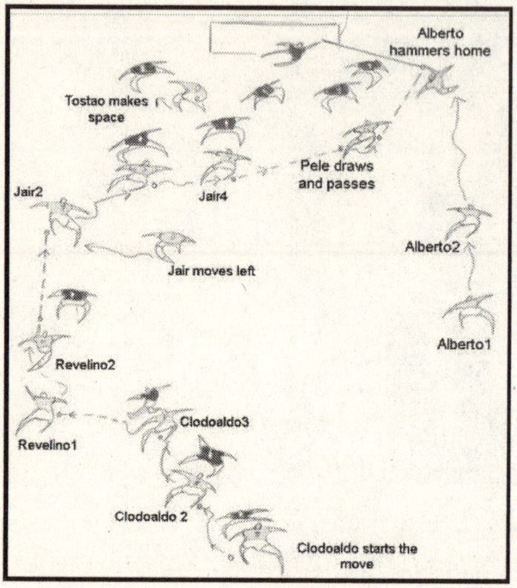

Carlos Alberto's iconic goal from the Final

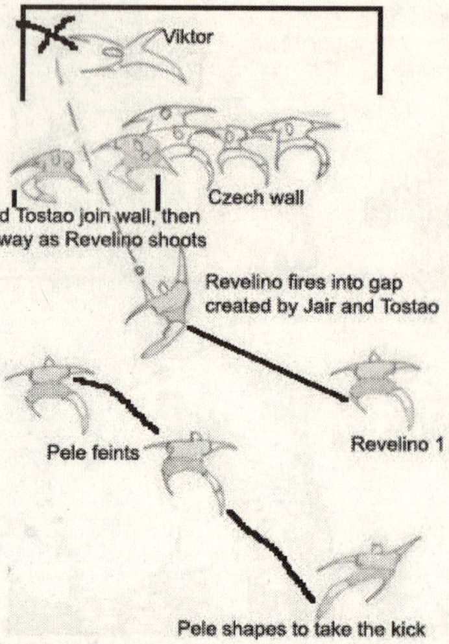

Rivellino's *Patada Atômica* free-kick

Pelé with Mário Zagallo

Australia debuts at the World Cup

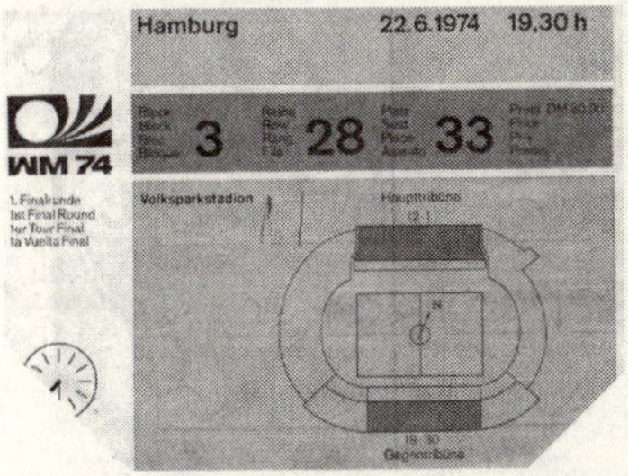

A sample ticket

Yugoslavia at the World Cup

Johan Cruyff at the final

The victorious West Germany team

West Germany players with the trophy

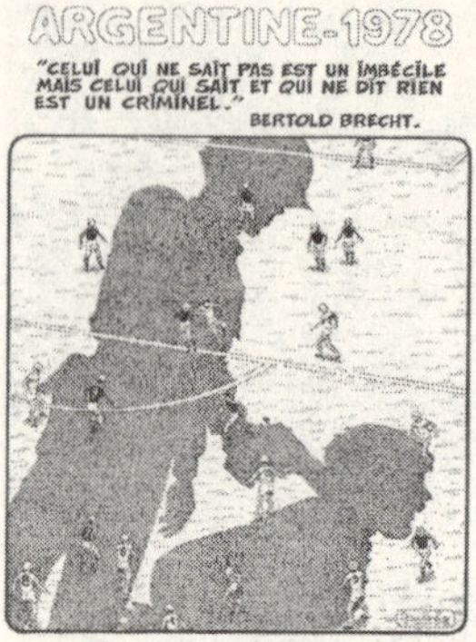

Posters highlighting dissent against the regime in Argentina as they hosted the World Cup

Opening ceremony of the 1978 World Cup

Tango Durlast: The official match ball

1982, SPAIN

STORIES

Maradona Against an Illusionary Wall

The match between Argentina and Belgium is largely remembered for a single frame of film rather than the scoreline. Captured by photographer Steve Powell at Barcelona's Camp Nou, the image of Diego Maradona, ball at his feet, facing down half a dozen Belgian defenders, is fondly recollected by many. The Belgians appear to be in a panicked, fan-like formation, frozen by the sheer presence of the 21-year-old maestro. It is an image that has come to symbolize Maradona's career: one man against the world.

However, the story behind the photograph is a fascinating study of how a single static frame can overshadow the reality.

To understand the photo, we must revisit the game. Contrary to the myth that Maradona had just completed a mazy run that left the defence in shambles, the scene was actually the aftermath of a free kick. The six Belgians in the frame – Franky Vercauteren, Ludo Coeck, Guy Vandersmissen, Luc Millecamps and Maurits De Schrijver – had formed a defensive wall.

When Osvaldo Ardiles tapped a short pass to Maradona, the wall broke apart. Powell's camera shutter clicked at the precise millisecond the wall began to disperse. Because of Powell's high vantage point and the use of a long lens, the pitch was flattened, making the defenders appear to be surrounding Maradona in a desperate tactical manoeuvre rather than simply running towards the ball.

The reality of the match was also far less romantic for Argentina. While the photo gives the impression of total control, Belgium's Antwerp defence actually managed to stifle Maradona for most of the game. Belgium won the match 1–0 thanks to a goal by Erwin Vandenbergh, marking a historic upset against the defending champions.

Doctor, Captain, Activist

There are few players more widely regarded as deserving of a World Cup than Brazil's captain at this edition, Sócrates, who never won one.

Known as 'O Doutor' (The Doctor) due to his medical degree, Sócrates viewed football not as an end in itself but as a means to propagate democracy in a country then strangled by military dictatorship.

His activism was rooted in a revolutionary movement he co-founded at his club, Corinthians, in São Paulo. Under this system, every decision was determined by a vote involving everyone from the janitors to the superstars. By the time the 1982 World Cup arrived, Sócrates brought this egalitarian spirit to the international stage. He famously wore headbands during the next edition (1986) with messages such as 'No Violence' and 'Need Justice', using the world's most-watched sporting event to signal to the people back home that the quest for freedom was as vital as the quest for a goal.

On the pitch, his style of play was an extension of his philosophy. Sócrates was a master of the no-look back-heel, a move that required a blind trust in his teammates and a refusal to conform to the rigid, physical tropes of European football. He and his teammates Zico, Falcão, and Toninho Cerezo played with a fluid, improvisational joy that became synonymous with '*jogo bonito*'.

To him, playing with such freedom while under a repressive regime was a defiant act of the soul. He believed that if the people could see beauty and democracy on the pitch, they would eventually demand the same principles in government.

While the tournament ended in heartbreak with a 3–2 loss to Italy, for Sócrates, the loss did not diminish the message. He famously expressed that he would rather lose playing the right way than win playing the wrong way, a sentiment that applied equally to his politics.

Disgrace of Gijón

The 'Disgrace of Gijón' remains the most cynical chapters in the history of the FIFA World Cup, a match so devoid of sporting integrity that it forced a permanent change to the laws of the game.

At El Molinón stadium in Gijón, Spain, on 25 June 1982, West Germany and Austria engaged in a pact of non-aggression that resulted in a 1–0 victory for the Germans. While the scoreline suggested a competitive edge, the reality was a manipulation that ensured both European powers progressed to the next round while intentionally eliminating Algeria.

The controversy was born from a scheduling flaw compounded by a major upset. Earlier in the group stage, Algeria had stunned West Germany 2–1, becoming the first African nation to beat a European team at a World Cup. By the time the final group match between West Germany and Austria kicked off, Algeria had already played their final game and sat in second place. Because of the staggered kick-off times, both West Germany and Austria knew exactly what was required: a German victory by one or two goals would see both teams through on goal difference, leaving Algeria in third place.

The match began with a deceptive intensity, and in the tenth minute, West German striker Horst Hrubesch scored the opening goal. With that goal, the mutually beneficial result had been achieved. For the remaining 80 minutes, the game descended into a farce that unsettled the 41,000 spectators in attendance. Players from both sides stopped tackling, refused to sprint and spent long stretches passing the ball aimlessly across their own backlines. The ball was frequently played back to goalkeepers, and any attacks were half-hearted gestures that never threatened the goal.

The reaction was one of universal outrage. Fans in the stands waved white handkerchiefs and chanted '*¡Fuera, fuera!*' (Out, out!). Infuriated Algerian fans at the stadium fences shook banknotes at the players, representing their belief that the match had been bought and sold. The broadcast booths were equally scathing; West German commentator Eberhard Stanjek eventually refused to commentate on the shameful display, while an Austrian announcer advised his viewers to turn off their television sets in protest.

Despite the obvious collusion, FIFA ruled that no official rules had been broken and allowed the result to stand. Algeria, the true victims of the afternoon, were sent home despite winning two of their three matches. However, the moral cost of the match was too high for FIFA to ignore. From that point forward, it was mandated that the final pair of matches in every group stage at major tournaments must be played simultaneously. This rule change, still in effect today, ensures that no team can play with the benefit of knowing their rival's final result.

Tragedy of Seville

The semi-final between France and West Germany has been iconised with the moniker 'Tragedy of Seville'. Played on 8 July 1982, at the Ramón Sánchez Pizjuán Stadium, it remains one of the most dramatic matches in the history of the World Cup.

The French team, led by the 'magic square' midfield of Michel Platini, Alain Giresse, Jean Tigana and Bernard Genghini, played with elegance. While West Germany, by contrast, represented a more relentless, physical pragmatism. The sides were level at 1–1 in the second half when the match's most infamous moment occurred. French substitute Patrick Battiston chased a lofted through-ball from Platini, beating the German goalkeeper, Harald

Schumacher, to the ball. Schumacher, showing no intent to play the ball, launched himself into the air and collided violently with Battiston's head.

Battiston was knocked unconscious, losing three teeth and suffering a damaged vertebra. As Platini held his friend's limp hand, many feared the player had died on the pitch. In an era before VAR, Dutch referee Charles Corver failed to award even a foul, let alone the red card and penalty that the assault clearly merited. To the fury of the French, Schumacher was allowed to remain on the pitch, where he stood impatiently on the goal line, seemingly indifferent to the carnage he had caused.

The injustice of the moment fuelled an extraordinary period of extra time. The French, galvanized by a sense of righteous indignation, surged into a 3–1 lead with stunning goals from Marius Trésor and Alain Giresse. With only 15 minutes remaining, France seemed destined for their first World Cup final. However, the Germans refused to break. Led by Karl-Heinz Rummenigge, playing despite a leg injury, the Germans clawed back to 3–3, forcing the first-ever penalty shoot-out in World Cup history. In the cruel lottery of the spot-kicks, Schumacher – the man who many felt should not have remained on the field – became the hero, saving two penalties to send West Germany to the final and ending France's dream of a maiden appearance there.

Rossi's Redemption

The story of Paolo Rossi at the 1982 World Cup in Spain is one of football's ultimate comeback stories.

The context of this triumph lies in what preceded it. In 1980, Rossi was embroiled in the Totonero match-fixing scandal. Although he vehemently denied the charges, he was banned from football for years. His suspension ended just weeks before the World Cup began, and his selection by manager Enzo Bearzot was met with protests from the Italian media. Critics argued that Rossi was physically frail, mentally rusty and an insult to more deserving players. For the first four games of the tournament, the criticism appeared justified. Rossi looked off pace and out of ideas as Italy scraped through the first round with three uninspired draws, with Rossi failing to find the net in any of them.

That changed on 5 July 1982, at the Estádio de Sarrià in Barcelona. Italy faced a Brazilian side that is still regarded as one of the greatest collections of talent ever assembled. The Seleção Canarinho – nickname for the Brazilain team – needed only a draw to advance while the Italians needed a miracle. In the match later known as the Tragedy of the Sarrià, Rossi finally showed the world his real capabilities, scoring a clinical hat-trick.

With his confidence restored, he became unstoppable. In the semi-final against Poland, he scored both goals in a 2–0 victory, and then in the final against West Germany at the Santiago Bernabéu stadium in Madrid, he scored the crucial opening goal, a diving header that set the stage for Italy's 3–1 triumph. In less than a week, Rossi had scored six goals against the three strongest teams in the tournament.

He thus finished the World Cup as the winner of the Golden Boot and the Golden Ball, and later that year, he was awarded the Ballon d'Or, completing a remarkable turnaround in fortune.

QUIZ

Questions

Kick-Off

1. Which team defeated El Salvador 10–1 at this edition, thus equaling the largest margin of victory in a World Cup match ever?
2. This was the first World Cup to feature the expanded 24-team format. An unprecedented instance of teams from all six continents thus occurred. Which were the two countries

from Asia and Oceania that made their tournament debut and contributed to this feat?

3. Who captained Italy at the age of 40 to a World Cup win, thus becoming the oldest winner of the tournament? This iconic talisman still holds that record.
4. Which was the only team not to progress beyond the first round of the group stage despite remaining unbeaten? (Italy qualified despite accumulating the same number of points due to a better goal-scoring record.)
5. Elba de Padua Lima, better known as Tim, was Peru's 67-year-old coach at the tournament and had played in the World Cup 44 years earlier. Which team did he represent at the 1938 edition in Italy?

Extra-Time

6. In the match between France and Kuwait, Alain Giresse scored a goal that was heavily contested by not just the Kuwaiti team but also saw Sheikh Fahad Al-Ahmad Al-Jaber Al-Sabah, president of their football association, march onto the pitch. What was the Kuwaiti players' complaint that made the referee change his mind and later disallow the goal?
7. In what is considered as one of the greatest matches in tournament history, West Germany beat France 5–4 in the first-ever World Cup penalty shoot-out in the semi-finals. Which player scored the decisive goal?
8. In one of the ugliest incidents of the tournament, which goalkeeper collided with France's Patrick Battiston, his right hip contacting Battiston's face and knocking him unconscious? The collision left Battiston with a couple of lost teeth, a damaged vertebra and temporarily in a coma.
9. Two iconic stadiums were key to Spain hosting the World Cup successfully. If the first hosted the most games, the latter was the designated final venue. Name both.

10. Who was the star of the Polish team that won a bronze medal at this FIFA World Cup, who scored four goals but missed the semi-final defeat to eventual champions Italy because he was suspended after being booked in the 88th minute of a 0–0 draw against the Soviet Union?

Shoot-Out

11. Which player scored England's fastest World Cup goal at this edition, netting just 27 seconds into their game against France?
12. Name Algeria's captain at this World Cup, who unfortunately was executed a decade later, in 1992, during a government crackdown on fundamentalists.
13. Defending champions Argentina didn't fare as expected – first losing against the Italians and then suffering a 3–1 defeat at the hands of Brazil. Which stadium hosted the latter match against their arch-rivals – a venue they were expected to win at, considering their marquee player had just signed for the club that called the ground home?
14. Name the Italian player who scored the last goal for the champions in the final. He also scored the first goal of the 1986 World Cup, thus becoming the first and, so far, only player to score in the final of one World Cup and in the opener of the next edition.
15. *Volver a Empezar* is a 1982 Spanish film which won the Academy Award for Best Foreign Language Film at the 55th Academy Awards. Which stadium was part of the film shot in, the visuals thus providing people a glimpse of the preparations for the world cup?

Word Search

As the World Cup expanded to 24 teams, an unprecedented 14 from a single continent (Europe) participated in the 1982 edition. Search through the puzzle to name those countries.

M	J	N	O	R	T	H	E	R	N	I	R	E	L	A	N	D	Y
H	U	Y	F	X	G	P	O	L	A	N	D	C	W	W	E	B	Y
J	R	G	G	W	E	S	T	G	E	R	M	A	N	Y	N	E	U
S	C	Z	E	C	H	O	S	L	O	V	A	K	I	A	G	L	G
D	C	A	S	O	V	I	E	T	U	N	I	O	N	U	L	G	O
Y	R	O	L	T	M	Y	D	G	Z	A	J	I	F	S	A	I	S
X	D	A	T	V	A	V	M	Z	G	K	N	O	R	T	N	U	L
Y	E	P	O	L	L	K	E	X	B	J	V	R	A	R	D	M	A
U	F	D	P	T	A	H	U	N	G	A	R	Y	N	I	X	R	V
D	S	P	A	I	N	N	M	J	M	W	K	P	C	A	C	I	I
C	V	A	K	Y	U	D	D	H	F	B	H	R	E	K	Z	I	A
K	W	X	P	P	W	O	X	I	T	A	L	Y	F	C	R	X	S

Find the following words in the puzzle.
Words are hidden →, ↓, and ↘.

NORTHERN IRELAND
CZECHOSLOVAKIA
SOVIET UNION
WEST GERMANY
YUGOSLAVIA
SCOTLAND
AUSTRIA
BELGIUM
ENGLAND
HUNGARY
FRANCE
POLAND
ITALY
SPAIN

ANSWER KEY

Answers to Questions

1. Hungary
2. Kuwait and New Zealand
3. Dino Zoff
4. Cameroon (England also suffered the same fate but they were eliminated after the second round of group stage.)
5. Brazil
6. Someone had whistled from the stands.
7. Horst Hrubesch
8. Harald Schumacher

9. Nou Camp and Santiago Bernebau
10. Zbigniew Boniek
11. Bryan Robson
12. Salah Assad
13. Nou Camp (Maradona had signed for FC Barcelona.)
14. Alessandro Altobelli
15. El Molinón in Gijón

Solution to Word Search

.	.	N	O	R	T	H	E	R	N	I	R	E	L	A	N	D	.
.	.	.	.	.	.	P	O	L	A	N	D	.	.	.	E	B	Y
.	.	.	.	W	E	S	T	G	E	R	M	A	N	Y	N	E	U
S	C	Z	E	C	H	O	S	L	O	V	A	K	I	A	G	L	G
.	C	.	S	O	V	I	E	T	U	N	I	O	N	U	L	G	O
.	.	O	.	.	.	.	.	.	.	.	.	.	F	S	A	I	S
.	.	.	T	.	.	.	.	.	.	.	.	.	R	T	N	U	L
.	.	.	.	L	.	.	.	.	.	.	.	.	A	R	D	M	A
.	.	.	.	.	A	H	U	N	G	A	R	Y	N	I	.	.	V
.	S	P	A	I	N	N	.	.	.	.	.	.	C	A	.	.	I
.	.	.	.	.	.	.	D	.	.	.	.	.	E	.	.	.	A
.	.	.	.	.	.	.	.	I	T	A	L	Y	.	.	.	.	.

Word directions and start points are formatted: (Direction, X, Y)

NORTHERN IRELAND (E,3,1)
CZECHOSLOVAKIA (E,2,4)
SOVIET UNION (E,4,5)
WEST GERMANY (E,5,3)
YUGOSLAVIA (S,18,2)
SCOTLAND (SE,1,4)
AUSTRIA (S,15,4)
BELGIUM (S,17,2)
ENGLAND (S,16,2)
HUNGARY (E,7,9)
FRANCE (S,14,6)
POLAND (E,7,2)
ITALY (E,9,12)
SPAIN (E,2,10)

1986, MEXICO

STORIES

Reach Early, Acclimatize Well

The 1986 World Cup presented a physiological challenge unlike any other edition of the tournament. Venues were located at altitudes ranging from of 500 to over 2,600 metres above sea level, often in temperatures exceeding 30°C, and because of broadcast commitments, most games kicked off around noon or in the afternoon.

To tackle these conditions, specifically to adapt to the sparse oxygen in the air, which could lead to rapid fatigue and dizziness, teams went to great lengths to acclimatize themselves before the tournament.

The most common strategy was early arrival. Medical consensus suggested that a minimum of 21 days was required for the body to produce the necessary haemoglobin levels to compete effectively.

Setting the trend was England, who under Bobby Robson, arrived in Mexico nearly a month early, setting up camp in the sweltering heat of Monterrey. Despite the preparation, the players struggled immensely with stomach illnesses and the sheer dehydration caused by the dry mountain air.

Defending champions Italy took a meticulous approach too, arriving early to train in the high-altitude regions. However, critics later argued they over-trained, leaving the players physically 'flat' by the time the knockout rounds began.

For many European nations, finding an environment that mimicked Mexico's unique combination of altitude and heat was difficult.

Franz Beckenbauer took his West Germany team to high-altitude camps in the Alps before flying to Mexico. Their strategy focused on intermittent hypoxic training, essentially forcing the body to work in oxygen-deprived conditions to build stamina. This paid off, as the Germans got better in the later stages of matches, reaching the final.

France too utilized sophisticated medical monitoring, checking blood oxygen levels daily to ensure players weren't over-exerting themselves during the adaptation phase.

South American teams, particularly those from the Andean regions, had a natural advantage, but they didn't leave it to chance either. Argentina's coach, Carlos Bilardo, a doctor by trade, moved the squad to Mexico well in advance and chose training sites specifically for their gruelling conditions. He also famously experimented with different diets to combat the altitude-induced nausea.

The Mexican Wave

The 'Mexican wave' is a collective act by spectators in a stadium who stand up progressively to give the illusion of a wave passing through the stands. It was originally popularized in the late 1970s and early 1980s in the United States. Professional cheerleader 'Krazy' George Henderson is widely credited with its first televised appearance on 15 October 1981, during a play-off game between the Oakland Athletics and the New York Yankees. Simultaneously, the University of Washington Huskies popularized a collegiate version just weeks later.

By 1984, it had become famous, most notably in Mexico, appearing at Estadio Universitario in Monterrey during a match between Mexico and Argentina. The 1986 World Cup, however, made it famous internationally. Since the tournament was broadcast globally, it was the first time viewers outside North America witnessed thousands of fans standing and sitting in a synchronized rhythm.

For television audiences, it quickly became associated with the colour and noise of Mexican stadiums such as the Estadio Azteca. This association led English-speaking countries outside North America to dub it the 'Mexican Wave', and the name stuck.

Today, it is replicated across stadiums all over the world but it all started with enthusiastic crowds at this edition of the World Cup showing the way!

Hand of God

The 'Hand of God' goal is perhaps the most controversial moment in the history of football. Occurring six minutes into the second half of the England vs Argentina quarter-final on 22 June 1986, the goal was more than just a sporting violation; it was a moment of profound cultural and political theatre that cemented Diego Maradona's legacy as a genius, both revered and reviled.

To understand the weight of the goal, it is worth remembering that the match took place against the backdrop of the Falklands War between Argentina and the United Kingdom, which had ended only four years earlier. For the Argentine public and Maradona himself, the game was a matter of national pride and symbolic revenge for the lives lost in the conflict. The atmosphere at the Estadio Azteca in Mexico City was thick with this unspoken tension.

The game itself lacked intensity until Argentina's number 10 made a surging run towards the English box in the 51st minute. He attempted a one-two pass with teammate Jorge Valdano, but the ball was intercepted by English midfielder Steve Hodge. In an attempt to clear the ball, Hodge inadvertently hooked it high into the air towards his own goal.

Maradona was dwarfed by the English goalkeeper Peter Shilton, and as the ball dropped, both men leaped. Physically, Shilton should have easily punched the ball clear. Instead, Maradona raised his left arm and punched the ball past the stranded goalkeeper into the net.

Despite the frantic protests of the English defenders, the goal was awarded.

In the post-match press conference, Maradona explained the goal in words that would become infamous. He described it as being scored 'a little with the head of Maradona, and a little with the hand of God.'

Linekar's Surge

Before he became the face of British sports broadcasting, Gary Lineker's career hung on a knife-edge in the sweltering heat of Mexico. Entering this World Cup, he was under immense scrutiny, coming off a six-match international goal drought that seemed to mirror England's own stuttering form. And after a loss to Portugal and a dismal draw against Morocco, he and England arrived at their final group match against Poland facing the ignominious prospect of elimination at the group stage.

It was at this point of the tournament that the then Everton striker exploded into life with a first-half hat-trick, propelling his country into the knockout stages and fundamentally altering the trajectory of his life.

The momentum from that afternoon in Monterrey proved unstoppable – he followed up with a brace against Paraguay, suddenly transforming from a struggling striker into the leading contender for the Golden Boot.

Even in the heartbreak of the quarter-final exit to Argentina, he managed to find the net one final time. That sixth goal clinched the Golden Boot, making him the first Englishman ever to receive the honour. The transformation was complete: Lineker went entered summer as a question mark and emerged as hot property, securing a high-profile £2.8 million move to FC Barcelona shortly after the tournament.

He went on to enjoy an illustrious international career, finishing as his country's highest goalscorer at World Cups and inducted into the English Football Hall of Fame, and it all started during that game against Poland in Monterrey.

Danish Dynamite

The Denmark team in this tournament was a special bunch. Affectionately known as 'Danish Dynamite', they had come into the tournament on the back of a fantastic European campaign two years earlier and, in Mexico, under alien conditions, put on a performance that made the world sit up and take notice.

Led by the pioneering German coach Sepp Piontek, they successfully fused tactical discipline with a unique sense of freedom and flair. The team operated in a fluid 3-5-2 system that prioritized attacking transitions and individual expression.

At the heart of this 'Dynamite' was a golden generation of talent. It featured Michael Laudrup, then just 21 and already a generational genius, and the explosive Preben Elkjær, a striker of immense power and technical skill who famously finished the tournament with a hat-trick and a reputation as one of the world's best. And it was supported by a cast of elite European professionals, including the tireless Søren Lerby, the inventive Frank Arnesen and the legendary libero Morten Olsen who dictated play from the back with the composure of a grandmaster. Together, the team was a well-oiled unit.

Their legend was forged in the opening round, where they were drawn into what was dubbed the first-ever 'Group of Death' alongside West Germany, Uruguay and Scotland. Far from being intimidated, the Danes dismantled the competition.

They opened with a gritty 1–0 win over Scotland and then followed this with a 6–1 annihilation of reigning South American champions Uruguay, which included Laudrup scoring one of the greatest solo goals in tournament history.

In their final group game, they defeated title favourites West Germany 2–0, thus winning all three group matches.

In the Round of 16 against Spain, Denmark again took an early lead through a Jesper Olsen penalty and looked destined for the quarter-finals. However, a catastrophic unforced error changed the course of the match.

In the 43rd minute, Jesper Olsen played a blind back-pass across his own penalty area, gifting a goal to Spain's Emilio Butragueño. The mistake, which gave birth to the Danish idiom '*en rigtig Jesper Olsen*' (a real Jesper Olsen), crushed the team's morale, and they just couldn't recover from the slump.

In the second half, the Danes over-committed to the attack in an 'all-or-nothing' gamble, leaving their defence exposed. Spain ruthlessly picked them apart on the counter-attack, winning 5–1 and thus ending the Nordic country's fairy-tale run.

QUIZ

Questions

Kick-Off

1. Which South American country was originally supposed to host the tournament but had to withdraw because of existing economic turmoil it faced in the early part of the decade? Hopes of an open selection for finding a replacement were all but ended when FIFA president João Havelange headed straight from the 1982 final to Mexico and later awarded the country their second World Cup in 16 years.
2. Which Asian team qualified for the tournament despite not playing a single qualifier at home due to a geopolitical war with a neighbouring nation?
3. What was the name of Paraguay's coach during their game against Belgium, who was sent off after he repeatedly entered the pitch?
4. Who was the Uruguay defender who received the fastest red card in FIFA World Cup history, having been sent off after

just 56 seconds against Scotland on 13 June 1986? French referee Joël Quiniou dismissed him for a reckless challenge on Gordon Strachan, forcing Uruguay to play with 10 men for the remainder of the 0–0 group-stage draw.

5. Which Spanish player scored four times in their 5–1 victory against Denmark, becoming the first player since Eusébio in 1966 to score four goals in a single World Cup match?

Extra-Time

6. Diego Maradona scored the 'Goal of the Century' against England in their quarter-final, dribbling 60 yards in 10 seconds. He bypassed Peter Beardsley, Peter Reid, Terry Fenwick, Peter Shilton and which other defender twice before scoring?
7. Which team became the first from Africa, and only the second nation from outside Europe and the Americas (after North Korea in 1966), to reach the second round? They did so by topping their group, which also included Poland, England and Portugal.
8. Which legendary Brazilian missed a penalty in regulation time as they went down to France in the quarter-finals? They eventually lost 4–3 on penalties.
9. Pique was the official mascot for the 1986 FIFA World Cup hosted in Mexico. It featured a large moustache, a Colima-style sombrero (the traditional Mexican cowboy hat), and green, white and red colours to represent the host nation. Its name derived from *picante* (Spanish for spicy) and PK (penalty kick). Which edible item was it meant to depict (the only instance of a food item chosen as a World Cup mascot)?
10. Which team's troubled time at the 1986 World Cup has come to be remembered as the Saltillo affair? Headquartered in the city of Saltillo during the tournament, they had experienced intense infighting, including a suspected doping case, player strikes and disputes with their national federation, marking a tumultuous campaign.

Shoot-Out

11. What unique but unwanted distinction did Franz Beckenbauer achieve at this edition, one that he later overcame in the 1990 World Cup?
12. Featuring elaborate design inspired by the host nation's native architecture, what was the official ball called – a name that it shared with the venue of the final?
13. Name the Argentine forward who scored the winner in the World Cup final. He had famously played in India during the 1984 Nehru Cup in Kolkata as part of Argentina's preparation for the 1986 World Cup and featured at Eden Gardens alongside teammates Nery Pumpido and Ricardo Giusti, narrowly defeating the Indian national team 1–0.
14. In one of the greatest matches of the tournament, Belgium defeated the Soviet Union 4–3 in the Round of 16. Which future Ballon d'Or winner scored a hat-trick for the losing Soviet side?
15. In Argentina's qaurter-final against England, Ali Bin Nasser was the referee who allowed Diego Maradona's controversial 'Hand of God' goal. When questioned later, he admitted he was waiting for a signal from his linesman. What was the name of the Bulgarian linesman who missed the incident?

Anagrams

Five different players found the back of the net in the final of the 1986 World Cup. Unscramble the following to name them.

Note: Diacritics such as accents or tildes have been omitted.

1. LOWERSUBJOINS
2. LODGERNAVAJO
3. ALZHEIMERGUNKMERING
4. LURIDVELOR
5. AUGSBURGCHARLIEJOUR

ANSWER KEY

Answers to Questions

1. Colombia
2. Iraq
3. Cayetano Re
4. José Batista
5. Emilio Butragueño
6. Terry Butcher
7. Morocco
8. Zico
9. A jalapeño pepper
10. Portugal
11. First to lose a World Cup final as both as a player (1966) and as a coach (1986), a distinction he overcame by winning the tournament as manager in 1990.
12. Azteca
13. Jorge Burruchaga
14. Igor Belanov
15. Bogdan Dochev

Solutions to Anagrams

1. José Luis Brown
2. Jorge Valdano
3. Karl-Heinz Rummenigge
4. Rudi Völler
5. Jorge Luis Burruchaga

1990, ITALY

STORIES

Gazza's Tears

The most enduring image of Italia'90, this edition of the World Cup, is not a goal or a trophy lift, but a close-up of a 23-year-old from Newcastle upon Tyne with red-rimmed eyes and a quivering lip.

Paul 'Gazza' Gascoigne's tears during the semi-final against West Germany transformed him from a talented athlete into a cultural icon, signalling a profound shift in the emotional landscape of English football.

By the time England reached the semi-final in Turin, 'Gazzamania' had already swept through Italy. Gazza was the heartbeat of Bobby Robson's side, a player of rare, intuitive genius who played with the infectious joy of a child in a schoolyard. However, his temperament was as fragile as his talent was robust. In the 99th minute of a tense 1–1 deadlock, he lunged for a ball and mistimed his tackle on Thomas Berthold. The referee, José Roberto Wright, reached for his pocket.

The yellow card was Gazza's second of the tournament, meaning that even if England progressed, he would be suspended for the final. The realization was instantaneous. While most players might have reacted with anger or stoic resignation, Gazza's face crumpled. As Gary Lineker famously looked towards the bench and gestured for someone to have a word with the distraught youngster, the cameras captured Gazza pulling his white England jersey up over his mouth to hide his sobbing.

When England eventually lost on penalties, the focus was not on tactical failure, but on the heartbreak of the boy who wouldn't get to play in the final. He wasn't demonized for the defeat; instead, he was greeted by 3,00,000 people at Luton Airport upon the team's return.

The beautiful game knew how to lift the fallen, and its sometimes brash, sometimes volatile son had just experienced that first-hand after what was a heartbreaking exit.

Totò Shines Brightest

Entering the World Cup, Totò Schillaci wasn't a key member of the host nation's squad. The 25-year-old had only made his international debut a few months earlier and, rather expectedly, began the tournament on the bench. Italy's manager, Azeglio Vicini, favoured established stars like Gianluca Vialli and Andrea Carnevale. However, in the opening match against Austria, the Azzurri found themselves frustrated by a stubborn defence. In the 74th minute, Vicini turned to the energetic Juventus forward. Just four minutes later, Schillaci rose to meet a cross from Gianluca Vialli, heading home the winning goal.

What followed was a phenomenon often described as *notti magiche* (magic nights), a phrase used to describe the euphoric atmosphere during this edition of the World Cup, later immortalized by the tournament's official song. Schillaci didn't just score; he stamped his authority as Italy won six of their games. His eyes, bulging with a mixture of disbelief and predatory hunger after every goal, reflected the raw passion of the Italian fans.

As the tournament progressed, Schillaci's scoring became prolific. He found the net against Czechoslovakia in the final group game, struck again in the Round of 16 against Uruguay, and scored the only goal in a tense quarter-final against Ireland. By the time the semi-finals arrived, 'Totò' was the first name on the team sheet, having displaced the world's most expensive players through sheer force of will.

Even in Italy's penalty shoot-out loss to Argentina in the semi-final, he scored his fifth goal of the tournament. He added a sixth from the penalty spot in the third-place play-off against England, securing the Golden Boot.

Spit-Fire

The clash between West Germany and the Netherlands in the Round of 16 is remembered for a bizarre, phlegm-filled meltdown between Frank Rijkaard and Rudi Völler.

The incident began in the 22nd minute with a late, cynical tackle by Rijkaard on Völler. As the referee, Juan Carlos Loustau, showed Rijkaard a yellow card, the Dutchman spat into Völler's iconic permed hair. The West German, understandably incensed, complained to the referee, only to be cautioned himself for his protests.

The chaos escalated just moments later. From the resulting free kick, Völler lunged for the ball that was safely in the hands of Dutch goalkeeper Hans van Breukelen. Rijkaard took exception to the challenge, grabbing Völler by the ear and stomping on his foot. In the ensuing scuffle, the referee decided to send both players off.

As they walked towards the touchline, the cameras captured the most famous image of the saga: Rijkaard, trailing behind Völler, calmly and deliberately spitting into the German's hair for a second time. It was a shocking breach of sporting etiquette that left Völler looking bewildered and the global audience in disbelief.

Rijkaard later admitted he was going through a difficult period in his personal life and was under immense stress. The high-stakes environment of the World Cup only intensified his frustration. He had done enough damage though, especially to Völler, who was largely the victim in this case. Yet Völler was sent off and suspended for the quarter-final, a decision the referee later admitted was a mistake born of confusion in the heat of the moment.

Score a Goal! Fetch a Rolls-Royce!

Making their first-ever World Cup appearance, the UAE arrived in Italy as rank outsiders. Drawn into a daunting Group D alongside eventual champions West Germany, powerhouse Yugoslavia and a formidable Colombia, they were expected to do little.

Perhaps to motivate the squad, a grand incentive was reportedly dangled by the UAE leadership: for every goal scored during the tournament, the scorer would be rewarded with a brand-new Rolls-Royce. The promise transformed the team's quest into a high-stakes hunt for individual and national glory.

In their second match against the clinical West Germans, the UAE found themselves trailing 2–0 in the mud. In the 46th minute, Khalid Ismaïl latched onto a defensive lapse and fired a powerful shot into the roof of the net. Though the UAE would eventually lose 5–1, Ismaïl's strike was a historic moment, the nation's first World Cup goal.

In the final group game against Yugoslavia, the feat was repeated. Ali Thani Juma'a found the net in a 4–1 defeat. The UAE exited the tournament with three losses and a goal difference of negative 9, yet they returned home to a hero's welcome.

The narrative of the luxury cars became a global fascination. However, like many great footballing myths, the reality of the Rolls-Royces was more nuanced than the legend suggests. In interviews decades later, players from the squad have offered conflicting accounts. Some, like Khalid Ismaïl, have confirmed receiving a luxury vehicle, while others have suggested the reward was a collective monetary prize rather than individual car keys.

Higuita Falters, Milla Latches

Back when it was extremely rare, Colombian custodian René Higuita was a pioneer of the 'sweeper-keeper' role. Known as El Loco (The Madman), Higuita was famous for his comfort on the ball, often dribbling past opposing strikers and playing short passes to his defenders. Throughout the 1990 group stages, this adventurous style had been an asset, helping Colombia build play from the back. However, in their Round of 16 fixture against Cameroon, he faltered.

The match had gone into extra time after a goalless 90 minutes. Roger Milla, coming off the bench, gave Cameroon the lead at 1–0 in the 106th minute. Desperate to equalize, Colombia pushed forward, and Higuita played even further out of his goal than usual. In the 109th minute, a back-pass was played to Higuita nearly 35 yards from his goal. Instead of clearing the ball, Higuita attempted to turn and dribble past Milla, who was closing him down with surprising speed for a 38-year-old man.

Milla had been warned by his former teammates at the French club Montpellier HSC – where Colombia's Carlos Valderrama also played – about the goalkeeper's habit of showboating. This time, he was ready. He tackled Higuita cleanly, stripped him of the ball, and found himself with an open goal before of him. Milla sprinted towards the goal and rolled the ball into the net to make it 2–0.

This goal helped Cameroon become the first African country ever to reach the quarter-finals of a World Cup.

QUIZ

Questions

Kick-Off

1. The selection of the host for this tournament is said to have been influenced by which famous sporting withdrawal? The decision was criticized heavily by the media from this country, which accused FIFA of political corruption and blamed the

organization's American sponsors (chiefly Coca-Cola) for influencing the vote.

2. The official draw for this edition of the World Cup was a star-studded affair. Which famous actress was one of the conductors along with television presenter Pippo Baudo, opera singer Luciano Pavarotti, and the then FIFA general secretary Sepp Blatter?
3. Name the 23-year-old Nigerian who died of heart failure during the 1990 World Cup qualifier against Angola.
4. For what unique (and rather unfathomable) reason did referee Michel Vautrot add an unwarranted eight minutes of first-half injury time to the semi-final between Italy and Argentina?
5. The Republic of Ireland advanced to the last eight without winning a match (other than on penalties), managing just two goals along the way. Who was their famous former World Cup–winning coach?

Extra-Time

6. In an amazing opening game, Cameroon defeated the defending champions Argentina with a goal from François Omam Biyik. What makes it more iconic is that their coach, Valery Nepomnyashchy, could not communicate with his team throughout the game. What logistical oversight contributed to this?
7. What unusual ritual did Argentina's goalkeeper at the 1990 World Cup, Sergio Goycochea, perform before leading his team in shoot-out wins against Yugoslavia and Italy? He later admitted to not being able to do the same in regulation time, as an Andreas Brehme penalty helped Germany win the tournament.
8. Which West German player, nicknamed the Magician of Köln, was playing in his second World Cup final at this edition? He

was in the squad for the 1986 World Cup too but was benched for the semi-finals and final.

9. A greeting in the local language of the host country, what was the name of the stick figure and football-headed mascot for this World Cup?
10. Despite inspiring performances from some underdogs, all previous World Cup winners – Argentina, England, Italy and West Germany – with eight previous titles between them, made it to the semi-finals. This was the second time in history that this happened – when was the previous such instance?

Shoot-Out

11. Tomáš Skuhravý scored five goals at this World Cup and finished as the second highest scorer in the tournament. His hat-trick against Costa Rica, though, was a first in tournament history – what was special about each of the three goals?
12. Name the Chilean goalkeeper who, during a qualifying match against Brazil, pretended to have been struck by a flare thrown from the crowd. For this act, his team was banned and did not qualify for the World Cup.
13. Roger Milla with his goals and signature celebration moves lit up the tournament. He, however, wasn't born with that name – what was his original surname? He changed it to Milla since he thought it sounded more African!
14. Robert Prosinečki scored World Cup goals for two different nations: while he helped Croatia to a historic third-place finish in 1998, which country did he represent at the 1990 tournament? His breakthrough performance earned him the FIFA Young Player Award.
15. The Stadio San Paolo played host to multiple games at this tournament, including the semi-final between Argentina and Italy. It was renamed in December 2020 to pay homage to someone who played in that game. What city is this ground in? Who was it named after?

Connect

Group the 16 commercial entities related to the 1990 World Cup into four groups of four. Each group shares a common connection. Each word belongs to one group only.

FIAT	CANON	IVECO	COCA-COLA
G-SHOCK	SNICKERS	ALITALIA	GILLETTE
ADIDAS	JVC	ALFA ROMEO	FUJIFILM
PHILIPS	BARILLA	BUDWEISER	VINI D'ITALIA

ANSWER KEY

Answers to Questions

1. USSR boycott of the 1984 Olympics
2. Sophia Loren
3. Samuel Okwaraji
4. He forgot to check his watch!
5. Jack Charlton
6. He wasn't provided with a translator. (The players couldn't speak Russian and he couldn't speak their mother tongue.)
7. He urinated on the pitch before penalty shoot-outs.
8. Pierre Littbarski
9. Ciao
10. 1970
11. All three were headers.
12. Roberto Rojas
13. Miller
14. Yugoslavia
15. Naples; Stadio Diego Armando Maradona named after Diego Maradona.

Solution to Connect

COCA-COLA	FUJIFILM	GILLETTE	JVC	*Official World Cup 1990 partners (global 'Official Sponsor' designation holders)*
ALITALIA	ALFA ROMEO	BARILLA	FIAT	*Italian national supporters*
CANON	PHILIPS	ADIDAS	G-SHOCK	*Equipment and broadcast technology brands associated with the tournament*
IVECO	SNICKERS	BUDWEISER	VINI D'ITALIA	*Brands featured on advertisement boards at the tournament*

1994, USA

STORIES

Divine Ponytail

Not every great World Cup story has a silver lining, and Roberto Baggio's outing at the 1994 FIFA World Cup is one of football's most heartbreaking tales. Entering the tournament as the reigning FIFA World Player of the Year and Ballon d'Or winner, and known as 'Il Divin Codino' – the Divine Ponytail – for both his talent and his hairstyle, he shouldered the expectations of an entire nation, and his performance in the USA remains the ultimate fairy tale that stopped just inches short of its destination.

Italy struggled through the group stage, suffering a shock 1–0 defeat to Ireland and barely advancing as one of the strongest third-placed teams. Baggio himself was quiet, but once the knockout stages began, he really came into his own against Nigeria. With his team trailing 1–0 and down to 10 men in the 88th minute, he struck a clinical equalizer to force extra time, where he then converted a penalty to secure a 2–1 win.

Then in a tense quarter-final, he rounded the Spanish goalkeeper to slot home the winner from a tight angle, sealing another 2–1 victory in the dying minutes of the game; he later came into his own again in the semi-final, scoring two magnificent first-half goals, the first a curling masterpiece after a deceptive dribble – to defeat a spirited Bulgarian side 2–1.

By the time Italy reached the final, he had scored 5 goals, accounting for nearly 71 per cent of Italy's knockout-round scoring.

The final against Brazil was a gruelling affair played in oppressive heat. The then-Juventus star, battling a hamstring strain sustained in the semi-final, was a shadow of his peak self but played the full 120 minutes.

The match ended 0–0, leading to the first-ever penalty shoot-out in a World Cup final. Baggio, the team's most reliable taker, stepped up for the fifth penalty. He had to score to keep Italy alive, but his shot famously sailed over the crossbar. The image of Baggio standing motionless, head bowed, while Brazil celebrated around him, became the tournament's most enduring image.

Attack, Don't Sit Back

Italia '90, the 1990 FIFA World Cup edition, had been widely criticized for its defensive, often cynical play, resulting in the lowest goals-per-game average in World Cup history (2.21). FIFA recognized this and introduced some transformative rule changes that were designed to penalize negativity and reward ambition.

The most notable tactical shift was the introduction of the back-pass rule. Prior to 1992, goalkeepers could pick up a ball intentionally kicked to them by a teammate. This allowed leading teams to waste time indefinitely, as defenders would simply roll the ball back to their keeper, who would hold it until pressured, only to repeat the cycle. By 1994, this safety net was gone. Goalkeepers were forced to use their feet, making them vulnerable to high-pressing strikers.

Teams were also incentivized to force a result. Before this edition, the standard group-stage reward for a victory was two points. In a two-point system, the mathematical incentive to risk a draw in pursuit of a win was low; a 0–0 stalemate was often seen as a 'good result' for both sides. The stakes were altered, with teams being awarded three points for a win and only one for a draw. The increased reward for a victory encouraged coaches to make attacking substitutions and take risks in the final 20 minutes of a match, as the gulf between one point and three points could define a tournament exit or progression to the next round.

Offside rules were also adjusted to favour the attacker. FIFA clarified that an attacker level with the second-to-last defender was onside. Previously, any doubt usually went to the defence, and being level was often flagged as an infraction. By giving the benefit of the doubt to the forward, through-balls and high defensive lines were encouraged, as strikers were given a split-second advantage to break towards the goal.

The results were for everyone to see; the tournament saw the goals-per-game average jump to 2.71, featuring high-scoring classics and a level of end-to-end drama that hadn't been seen in decades.

Diego's Scream

After a 15-month suspension for cocaine use in 1991, Diego Maradona arrived in the United States in peak physical shape, having lost 15 kilograms through an intense training regimen. However, his tournament ended abruptly on 30 June 1994, when a positive drug test for ephedrine resulted in his immediate expulsion.

As 1986 champions and defending runner-up, Argentina began the tournament as favourites, largely due to Maradona's revitalized form. On 21 June 1994, Maradona scored a spectacular goal in a 4–0 victory over Greece. The celebration however became infamous as he ran towards a sideline camera, eyes bulging, screaming in defiance. Those bloodshot eyes startled onlookers and perhaps suggested all was not well.

Four days later, he provided a crucial assist for Claudio Caniggia in a 2–1 win against Nigeria. Immediately following this match, a nurse famously led him off the pitch by the hand for a random doping test. The test revealed a 'cocktail' of five variants of ephedrine, a banned stimulant often found in weight-loss supplements or over-the-counter cold medicines.

While he claimed he took the substances unknowingly via a weight-loss drink that contained ephedrine, the organizers didn't relent and handed him a 15-month suspension. Devastated by the expulsion, Maradona famously stated, '*Me cortaron las piernas*' ('They have cut off my legs').

His exit shattered the Argentine team's morale and momentum. Without their captain, they lost their final group game to Bulgaria and were subsequently eliminated in the Round of 16 by Romania.

In many ways, it was the end of his glittering career; while he later returned to club football with Boca Juniors, he never played for Argentina again, with that match against Nigeria being his last in the national colours.

Bald Eagle from Bulgaria

Often referred to as The Magician, Yordan Letchkov was a gifted Bulgarian midfielder who became the face of a 'Golden Generation' that led their country to a historic semi-final appearance in the United States.

The east European team entered the tournament having never won a World Cup match in five previous attempts. Their campaign started poorly with a 3–0 loss to Nigeria, but the team, led by the fiery Hristo Stoichkov and the creative Letchkov, found their rhythm. Letchkov played an important role in their resurgence, scoring in a 4–0 thrashing of Greece and helping the team navigate the group stages to reach the knockout rounds.

He sealed his legacy on 10 July though, at Giants Stadium in New Jersey. Bulgaria faced the defending world champions, Germany. The match seemed to be following a familiar script when Letchkov committed a foul on Jürgen Klinsmann, leading to a German penalty and a 1–0 lead. However, the final 12 minutes saw the game turn on its head – first Stoichkov curled in a magnificent free kick to level the score at 1–1.

And then, just three minutes later, Zlatko Yankov sent a hopeful cross towards the penalty spot. Letchkov, showing incredible anticipation, sprinted past the diminutive Thomas Hässler and launched into a diving header. The ball flew past goalkeeper Bodo Illgner, sealing the win.

With his bald patch and the soaring header, he was christened the 'Bald Eagle' – quite fitting, given the tournament was being hosted in the United States!

A Disney Mascot

The mascot of World Cup USA '94 was Striker, an anthropomorphic dog, who became a ubiquitous symbol of the tournament's attempt to appeal to the local audience.

FIFA commissioned Warner Bros. Animation to design the mascot. This was the first time a major Hollywood studio was tasked with creating a World Cup identity.

The choice of a dog was deliberate. While other nations often chose animals with deep national symbolism (like the British Lion or the French Cockerel), the designers chose a dog simply because it was the most common and beloved domestic pet in the United States. Striker, wearing American colours, was designed to be approachable, friendly and non-threatening. He was intended to help demystify the sport for an American public that was still largely unfamiliar with it.

His name, too, was a direct nod to the most exciting position on the field, an ode to the theme for the tournament.

And because both Warner Bros. and Disney were involved, the merchandizing was unprecedented. Striker appeared on everything from Coca-Cola bottles to McDonald's Happy Meals, and he even had his own 'Striker's Soccer School' segments on television to teach kids the rules of the game.

QUIZ

Questions

Kick-Off

1. What was the name of the venue that became the first indoor stadium to host a World Cup match at this edition? To this day, it remains one of only three, along with Sapporo Dome (2002) and Arena AufSchalke (2006), to hold this distinction.
2. Which Colombian defender who had scored an own goal against the United States was shot to death when he returned home, possibly in retaliation for his mistake?
3. After winning the penalty shoot-out against Italy, the Brazilian team received the trophy from the then Vice President of the United States, Al Gore. Who did they then collectively decide to dedicate the win to, someone who had lost his life just a few months earlier?
4. The opening ceremony of this edition took place on 17 June at Chicago's Soldier Field. Name the musician who was supposed to take a ceremonial penalty kick before her performance, with the goal designed to split in two as part of a planned stunt, but instead managed to kick the ball wide. The goalposts collapsed anyway, leading to quite the comical sight.
5. When Cameroon played Russia, the game produced two individual goal-scoring records. Name the legend who, at the age of 42, became the oldest goalscorer in World Cup history, and also his opponent who scored five times, thus becoming the first – and so far only – player to hold that distinction?

Extra-Time

6. The legendary Diego Maradona had a tournament to forget, as he was sent back home after failing a drugs test. Which venue did he play both his games at, one that was the home ground of one of the most successful dynasties in the NFL and whose new stadium is set to host matches at the 2026 World Cup?

7. How did Brazilian defender Jorginho's injury during the final initiate a three-peat that is unique in the tournament's history?
8. Name the Italian custodian who became the first goalkeeper to be sent off from a game at the World Cup. Ironically, he was shown a red card for 'handling the ball' – he was outside his box.
9. Which player, brother of a former Brazilian legend, started this tournament by emulating his sibling and captaining the team but was later relegated to being a non-starter? He was replaced by Mazinho in the starting XI, and Dunga took over the captaincy as his team won their fourth World Cup title.
10. Which German midfielder was sent home after getting into an altercation with fans after being substituted against South Korea? He never represented his country again after this incident.

Shoot-Out

11. Which FIFA World Cup record holder, who served as the coach of the hosts at the 1994 edition, was honoured by the mascot for the recently concluded 2025 U-17 World Cup in Qatar?
12. Which Saudi Arabian and Al Hilal legend scored the first of his 3 goals spread across four editions of the World Cup during their match against Morocco at this tournament?
13. Only four players have scored multiple hat-tricks in the history of the World Cup. While Sandor Koscis, Just Fontaine and Gerd Muller all netted 2 goals at the same edition of the tournament, which player scored his first in 1994 and then repeated the feat four years later?
14. During the 1994 World Cup, this official later admitted that he failed to award a penalty when Thomas Helmer tripped Josip Weber in the penalty box against Germany – an error that cost him any further appointments at the tournament. This wasn't his only high-profile blip, as he was subsequently handed a lifetime ban following match-fixing allegations in the 1996–97 UEFA Champions League. Who was this referee?

15. Which national side, which is making a return to FIFA World Cup in 2026 after 18 years, has qualified for three FIFA World Cups previously, and have been eliminated by the same opposition in all three tournaments? 1994 was the edition in which they exited during the group stage, but their only loss came against this team, which had eliminated them in 1934 and would do the same in 1998.

Word Search

The final of this tournament ended goalless after regulation and extra time. Nine players ended stepping up to the penalty spot in the shoot-out. Search through the puzzle to name them.

L	S	M	I	M	F	R	A	N	C	O	B	A	R	E	S	I	I
J	V	P	V	H	P	P	I	U	I	Y	H	B	G	L	M	I	L
B	D	R	N	X	M	W	S	P	F	P	L	V	R	U	F	O	F
A	L	B	E	R	I	C	O	E	V	A	N	I	D	A	Z	K	K
D	E	M	E	T	R	I	O	A	L	B	E	R	T	I	N	I	Q
U	J	D	A	N	I	E	L	E	M	A	S	S	A	R	O	C	D
M	R	X	L	X	L	D	R	M	R	M	K	Q	K	T	C	M	O
Z	B	S	O	Q	H	O	F	Y	O	P	J	T	T	N	M	H	L
G	D	E	M	A	R	C	I	O	S	A	N	T	O	S	D	S	C
U	A	P	F	T	U	W	B	L	R	O	M	A	R	I	O	I	I
T	R	O	B	E	R	T	O	B	A	G	G	I	O	D	P	S	T
P	P	T	I	R	F	B	P	Z	D	U	N	G	A	G	C	Q	S

Find the following words in the puzzle.
Words are hidden →, ↓, and ↘.

DEMETRIO ALBERTINI
DANIELE MASSARO
ALBERICO EVANI
ROBERTO BAGGIO
MARCIO SANTOS
FRANCO BARESI
ROMARIO
BRANCO
DUNGA

ANSWER KEY

Answers to Questions

1. Pontiac Silverdome
2. Andrés Escobar
3. Ayrton Senna
4. Diana Ross
5. Roger Milla and Oleg Salenko
6. Foxboro Stadium, in Foxborough, Massachusetts. It was the home ground of the New England Patriots. (It has since been replaced by Gillette Stadium, which opened in 2002.)
7. Cafu was subbed in – in 2002, he became the first player to play in three World Cup finals.
8. Gianluca Pagliuca
9. Raí
10. Stefan Effenberg
11. Bora Milutinović
12. Sami Al-Jaber
13. Gabriel Batistuta
14. Kurt Röthlisberger
15. Norway

Solution to Word Search

.	.	.	.	.	F	R	A	N	C	O	B	A	R	E	S	I	.
.	.	.	.	.	.	.	.	.	.	.	.	B	.	.	.	.	.
.	.	.	.	.	.	.	.	.	.	.	.	.	R	.	.	.	.
A	L	B	E	R	I	C	O	E	V	A	N	I	.	A	.	.	.
D	E	M	E	T	R	I	O	A	L	B	E	R	T	I	N	I	.
.	.	D	A	N	I	E	L	E	M	A	S	S	A	R	O	C	.
.	.	.	.	.	.	.	.	.	.	.	.	.	.	.	.	.	O
.	.	.	.	.	.	.	.	.	.	.	.	.	.	.	.	.	.
.	.	.	M	A	R	C	I	O	S	A	N	T	O	S	.	.	.
.	.	.	.	.	.	.	.	.	R	O	M	A	R	I	O	.	.
.	R	O	B	E	R	T	O	B	A	G	G	I	O	.	.	.	.
.	.	.	.	.	.	.	.	.	D	U	N	G	A	.	.	.	.

Word directions and start points are formatted: (Direction, X, Y)

DEMETRIO ALBERTINI (E,1,5)
DANIELE MASSARO (E,3,6)
ALBERICO EVANI (E,1,4)
ROBERTO BAGGIO (E,2,11)
MARCIO SANTOS (E,4,9)
FRANCO BARESI (E,6,1)
ROMARIO (E,10,10)
BRANCO (SE,13,2)
DUNGA (E,10,12)

1998, FRANCE

STORIES

The Curious Case of Ronaldo

Ronaldo had lit up the 1998 FIFA World Cup with his brilliant finishing, having scored four goals leading up to the final. The game against France was supposed to be his coronation, but fate had different plans.

The drama began roughly four hours before kick-off at the Brazilian team's hotel. While his roommate Roberto Carlos looked on in horror, Ronaldo suffered a major seizure. He lost consciousness for several minutes and was reportedly foaming at the mouth. The Brazilian squad was traumatized, and Ronaldo was rushed to a clinic for neurological tests. Meanwhile, back at the stadium, the world received the shocking news. When the official team sheets were distributed to the media 72 minutes before kick-off, his name was missing. Edmundo was listed in his place.

The striker eventually arrived at the stadium just 45 minutes before the game began and claimed the medical tests had come back clear. He pleaded with coach Mário Zagallo to let him play, and was thus reinstated into the starting line-up.

However, he was a pale shadow of his usual self; appearing dazed, his movements sluggish and his legendary acceleration nowhere to be found. He famously collided with French goalkeeper Fabien Barthez early in the match, looking listless and disconnected.

France went on to win 3–0, securing their first-ever World Cup title. The images of Zidane's face projected onto the Arc de Triomphe defined the night for the French, but for the rest of the world, the marquee story was about the man who failed to deliver at the biggest night of his life.

The aftermath of the final triggered a parliamentary inquiry in Brazil. Conspiracy theories emerged: some claimed Nike allegedly pressured the team to play their superstar despite his health; others whispered of a secret pay-off to throw the game.

Medical experts later theorized that an injection of anaesthetic into Ronaldo's knee earlier in the day might have accidentally entered a vein, causing the seizure.

Ronaldo redeemed himself four years later, but the ghost of 1998 remains a smut in his otherwise spectacular career.

Beckham's Agony

A split-second lapse in judgement during a Round of 16 clash against Argentina transformed David Beckham into a national pariah. The red card he received exposed a terrible fan culture in England.

With the match tied at 2–2, early in the second half, Beckham was fouled from behind by the Argentine captain, Diego Simeone. As Simeone stood over him, he gave Beckham a shove to the back of the head.

Reacting in a moment of brashness rather than calculated malice, Beckham, still lying face-down on the turf, flicked his right leg upward, catching Simeone on the calf. It was soft contact, but it was still an intentional act of retaliation. Simeone collapsed to the ground with theatrical emphasis.

Danish referee Kim Milton Nielsen did not hesitate. He flashed a red card, dismissing the youngster and leaving England to play the remainder of the game with only ten men. England fought valiantly but eventually succumbed to their recurring nightmare: a loss on penalty kicks.

The reaction in England was venomous. Other moments in the match, like Sol Campbell's disallowed goal or the team's failure in the shoot-out, were all discarded in favour of a singular scapegoat. The *Daily Mirror* famously ran the headline: '10 Heroic Lions, One Stupid Boy.'

The abuse reached disturbing levels. An effigy of Beckham was hung from a lamp post outside a London pub, and he received numerous death threats. Every away stadium he visited during the following Premier League season greeted him with a deafening chorus of boos. For a year, Beckham was the most hated man in his own country.

Years later, Diego Simeone admitted to his role in the dismissal, confessing that he had exaggerated the contact to ensure Beckham was sent off, noting that the referee had been tricked.

Curse of the Goal Post

In 1990, playing on home soil, Italy was eliminated in the semi-finals by Argentina on penalties. In 1994, they reached the final, only for the world's best player, Roberto Baggio, to famously miss the last penalty.

So by the time the 1998 World Cup took place, the Italian public had developed a collective neurosis when it came to shoot-outs.

Their quarter-final against the hosts was a tactical stalemate. For 120 minutes, Italy and France traded blows without scoring. Roberto Baggio, seeking redemption for 1994, successfully converted his kick, exorcizing his personal demons. However, as the shoot-out progressed, the 'curse' manifested in its most literal form. Luigi Di Biagio stepped up to take the fifth penalty. If he missed, Italy was out.

Di Biagio struck the ball with power, aiming high and central. It beat the French goalkeeper, Fabien Barthez, but it didn't go in. Instead, it struck the underside of the crossbar. The Italian media thus began discussing the '*maledizione dei legni*' (the curse of the woodwork).

Some analysts claimed the unique architecture of the Stade de France roof created shifting shadows on the pitch that distorted the kickers' depth perception, while others blamed the Tricolore ball, claiming its synthetic layers made it more prone to rising off the foot.

Speculations galore, but curse or no curse, Italy became the first nation in history to be knocked out of three consecutive World Cups via a penalty shoot-out.

Super Eagles Fall Prey To Infighting

Nigeria arrived at the tournament not just as African champions, but as the reigning Olympic gold medalists from the 1996 Atlanta Games. Brimming with world-class players like Jay-Jay Okocha, Nwankwo Kanu and Sunday Oliseh, they began the tournament in breathtaking fashion. Their opening match against Spain is still regarded as one of the greatest upsets in World Cup history. Down 2–1, the Nigerians roared back to win 3–2. They followed this by beating Bulgaria 1–0, securing their place in the Round of 16 with a game to spare.

They looked set to progress further but, behind the scenes, there was growing unrest between the players and the Nigerian Football Federation. The conflict centred on unpaid match bonuses and allowances that had been promised to the players for their successful group-stage performance.

The night before their crucial Round of 16 knockout match against Denmark, things really got out of hand. Instead of resting and mentally preparing for the game, the players spent hours in the lobby of their hotel in a heated stand-off with officials. Reports from the time suggest the arguments lasted until the early hours of the morning. The players demanded their cash upfront, refusing to go to their rooms until they had received what they were owed.

The physical and psychological toll of the dispute was laid bare the following day at the Stade de France. Denmark, led by the Laudrup brothers, were a disciplined side, and from the opening whistle, the Super Eagles – nickname for the Nigerian team – looked like a shadow of themselves. They were sluggish and the trademark energy that had overwhelmed Spain was non-existent. Denmark scored after just three minutes and were 2–0 up by the 12th minute. Nigeria eventually lost 4–1, a humiliating exit for a team that was touted by many as having the talent to go much further in the tournament.

Tartan Army Invokes Joy

In June 1998, the dedicated travelling supporters of the Scottish national team, the Tartan Army, amazed the world with their presence at the World Cup. Their team was slated to play the opening match of the tournament against the defending champions Brazil, and while only about 7,000 Scots held official tickets for the match at the Stade de France, an estimated 20,000 to 30,000 fans descended upon Paris.

The sight was very different from anything the French capital had seen. Thousands of men in kilts, faces painted with the St Andrew's Cross, occupied popular hangouts in the French capital. They brought about a carnival-like atmosphere unlike any other across the different host cities. The defining characteristic of the Tartan Army in 1998 was their relentless optimism. Despite Scotland losing 2–1 to Brazil (due to a heartbreaking own goal) and eventually being eliminated in the group stage after a 3–0 loss to Morocco, the fans never turned sour.

Their behaviour was so exemplary that the French government and the local organizing committee praised them publicly. In an era where hooliganism was common and fans were often viewed as a security threat to be managed by riot police, the Scots were welcomed into bars and homes.

The impact of the Scottish supporters was so noteworthy that they were eventually awarded the 'Best Supporters' title by the French authorities and FIFA. There was even a shoutout given within the European Parliament to recognize the Tartan Army as a model for how sports fans should conduct themselves abroad.

QUIZ

Questions

Kick-Off

1. Who was sent off in the 70th minute of the group-stage match against Saudi Arabia for a stamp on Fuad Anwar, thus becoming the first player from his country to receive a red card at the World Cup? Hint: He received an even more infamous red card in a World Cup a few years later.
2. Which legendary defender, who played 142 games for France, only scored in one, but that happened to be the semi-final of this tournament against Croatia?
3. Which Iranian player scored the winning goal as the Asian team registered their first-ever World Cup win against the USA amidst political unrest between the two countries?
4. What name was given to the mascot of this tournament, one that was picked by television viewers and formed as a portmanteau of the sport with a suffix inspired by a popular French comic book series?
5. Which player who later appeared in the film *The Theory of Everything* thus became the first to hold this rare distinction of having won a World Cup as well as appeared in an Academy Award–nominated film?

Extra-Time

6. In an interview decades later, former Union of European Football Associations (UEFA) president and the 1984 UEFA European Football Championship (UEFA Euro 84) winner Michel Platini admitted that the draw for the tournament was rigged to keep two sides from meeting in the early stages of the tournament. Which two teams was this effort focused on benefitting?
7. Which player's goal from the quarter-final between Argentina and the Netherlands lit the tournament up? Controlling a long

pass instantly in the air, he wrong-footed a defender before rifling the ball into the roof of the net with the outside of his boot. Argentine custodian Carlos Roa could only look on as it sailed out of his reach.

8. Which European team's entire squad famously dyed their hair blonde during the tournament? The players had made a pact with coach Anghel Iordănescu. If they qualified for the knockout stages after only two group matches, the players would bleach their hair, and the coach would shave his head – they held on to their end of the deal!
9. In 2017, New Caledonia famously qualified for the Under-17 World Cup, hosted in India. A FIFA member since 2004, the island, with a population of just over 2,50,000, regarded it as a major achievement. But which famous player became, in 1998, the first to be born in this country and win the senior World Cup?
10. Who was the first player to score a golden goal in World Cup history at this tournament?

Shoot-Out

11. After France defeated Brazil, Arsenal manager Arsène Wenger handed a World Cup squad member an extra five days off. Who was this player, who consequently went to stay at a plush hotel in Monaco and ended up winning $28,000 on a slot machine?
12. There are two managers who are at helm of teams at the 2026 World Cup who have formerly won the tournament as captains. Interestingly, both played in the 1998 edition – if Didier Deschamps is one, which other World Cup–winning skipper (from 2006) is in charge of a team at the 2026 event?
13. Which goalkeeper, a star of France '98 and later in club football in England, turned to motorsports after retiring? He was crowned the national GT champion as well as drove in the prestigious Le Mans 24-Hour race.

14. Ahead of hosting the 1998 FIFA World Cup, France needed a new national stadium. After negotiations between Paris mayor Jacques Chirac and Prime Minister Édouard Balladur, it was decided that the new arena, the Stade de France, would be constructed in a specific neighbourhood in Paris. Decades later, the same locality would play a central role in the 2024 Olympic Games. Which locality is this?
15. From March to May 1998, a terror plot organized by Armed Islamic Group of Algeria and backed by Osama bin Laden was uncovered, and their efforts to harm the tournament were thwarted. Which particular game was uncovered to be the fixture that these groups were going to target?

Anagrams

The FIFA Technical Study Group announced an All-Star Team at the conclusion of the 1998 World Cup. Unscramble the following to name five of the players from that line up.

Note: Diacritics such as accents or tildes have been omitted.

1. AGRAARLMARCOS
2. ADBURLPURINA
3. HALEJILTERVISCOUS
4. KUDOSRAVER
5. GRIDDEDVASA

ANSWER KEY

Answers to Questions

1. Zinedine Zidane (also sent off in the 2006 World Cup final for his headbutt on Marco Materazzi)
2. Lilian Thuram
3. Mehdi Mahdavikia

4. Footix – combining 'foot' (from football) with the suffix '-ix', a nod to the Gaulish name style in the French comic series *Asterix*
5. Frank Leboeuf
6. France and Brazil
7. Dennis Bergkamp
8. Romania
9. Christian Karembeu
10. Laurent Blanc
11. Emmanuel Petit
12. Fabio Cannavaro (He is Uzbekistan's manager at the 2026 World Cup.)
13. Fabien Barthez
14. Saint-Denis
15. England vs Tunisia

Solutions to Anagrams

1. Carlos Gamarra
2. Brian Laudrup
3. José Luis Chilavert
4. Davor Šuker
5. Edgar Davids

2002, KOREA–JAPAN

STORIES

Scolari's Salvation Act

Following the loss to France in the 1998 final, the legendary Mário Zagallo stepped down as coach of Brazil. He was replaced by Vanderlei Luxemburgo, who initially found success by winning the 1999 Copa América. However, his tenure quickly soured due to inconsistent qualifying results, including shock losses to Chile and Paraguay and off-field scandals involving tax evasion. The final straw came in September 2000, when the Brazil side lost to Cameroon in the quarter-finals of the Sydney Olympics. He was sacked shortly afterwards, leaving the team fourth in the 10-team qualifying group.

In October 2000, the Brazilian Football Confederation (CBF) appointed Émerson Leão, a hardline disciplinarian and former national team goalkeeper. Leão's sought to prioritize domestic-based players, leaving the squad short on international experience in the squad, and that meant his stay was limited to just 11 matches. After a dismal showing at the 2001 Confederations Cup, where Brazil lost to Australia in the third-place play-off and won only one of five matches, he was reportedly told he would be sacked upon his return to Brazil; he resigned at the Tokyo airport in June 2001.

Luiz Felipe Scolari was subsequently appointed as the team was in genuine danger of missing the 2002 tournament. His start was equally rocky, losing to Uruguay and suffering a historic 2–0 elimination by Honduras in the 2001 Copa América. He responded, however, by switching to a 3-5-2 formation, providing defensive cover that allowed wing-backs Cafu and Roberto Carlos to attack.

The Seleção eventually secured third place in qualification. Entering the 2002 World Cup as underdogs, the team found its rhythm early and held on as they became the first to win all seven matches in a single tournament.

Fastest Goal and a Quick Fall From Grace

Hakan Şükür famously led Turkey to a third-place finish in this tournament. His personal campaign in particular reached a legendary conclusion during the third-place play-off against South Korea on 29 June 2002. Just 11 seconds after kick-off, he pounced on a defensive lapse to score the fastest goal in FIFA World Cup history. This record, which still stands in 2026, cemented his iconic status. He followed the goal with two assists in a 3–2 victory, securing Turkey's historic bronze medal.

The adoration Şükür once received contrasts sharply, however, with the social media frenzy that erupted years later when he was spotted working as an Uber driver in the United States. Following a political fallout with President Recep Tayyip Erdoğan and a subsequent arrest warrant related to a 2016 coup attempt – charges Şükür denies – his assets were seized, and he fled to Palo Alto, California.

Images of him driving around quickly spread online, and reports soon followed that he was also selling books to make ends meet. Fans worldwide reacted with a mixture of shock and sympathy, seeing a man with 51 international goals and a World Cup record now making ends meet by driving and selling books.

Not just that, the sensitivity surrounding him remains so high that, even in 2025 and 2026, Turkish media continues to face repercussions for mentioning his name. During the 2022 World Cup, commentator Alper Bakırcıgil was famously fired at half-time after simply noting that Şükür held the record for the fastest goal.

Oliver Kahn't Do No Wrong?

Germany was not considered one of the favourites leading up to this World Cup, yet Oliver Kahn's presence between the posts made them nearly impossible to beat. He kept five clean sheets in seven matches, conceding only a single goal during the first six games of the tournament.

Remarkably, he performed these feats while playing with a torn finger ligament.

His performances were especially exemplary in the knockout stages, where he made a string of spectacular saves to preserve 1–0 victories over Paraguay, the United States and South Korea.

The final against Brazil on 30 June 2002, was billed as a clash between the world's best attack and its greatest goalkeeper. For 66 minutes, Kahn held firm, but in the 67th minute, his tournament turned on its head. Rivaldo unleashed a speculative, long-range drive. It was a shot Kahn would normally have saved with ease, but he opted to catch the ball rather than parry it. The ball spilled off his chest directly into the path of Ronaldo, who swept the rebound into the net.

Brazil added a second goal 12 minutes later to win 2–0. As the final whistle blew, the image of a devastated Kahn slumped against his goalpost became the tournament's most poignant image.

Despite the fumble, the legendary goalkeeper's dominance was such that he had already been voted the Golden Ball winner before the final concluded. Perhaps the verdict of that poll would have been different had it been conducted after the final, but nothing could take away from the incredible month Kahn enjoyed in East Asia that summer.

Rivaldo's Gimmick

As Rivaldo delayed taking a corner in the dying minutes of Brazil's group fixture against Turkey, opposition defender Hakan Ünsal, visibly frustrated by the time-wasting, kicked the ball towards him.

Replays clearly showed the ball striking Rivaldo firmly on the shin or thigh. Despite the lack of contact with his head, Rivaldo collapsed to the turf, writhing around the corner flag and clutching his face in apparent agony. The South Korean referee, Kim Young-Joo, was deceived by the theatrics and showed Ünsal a second yellow card, resulting in his dismissal. As Ünsal walked towards the tunnel, the stadium's giant screen replayed the incident, exposing the Brazilian striker and sparking a chorus of boos from the crowd.

In the post-match fallout, Rivaldo admitted the ball did not hit his face but justified his actions by claiming he had used his experience to ensure Ünsal was punished for his initial nonchalant toe-poke. He famously remarked, 'My experience counts… I was both the victim and the person who got fined.‘

FIFA, however, did not take kindly to this. He became the first player punished under a new crackdown on simulation. He was fined 10,000 Swiss francsbut escaped a suspension, allowing him to play in the subsequent matches that led to Brazil's victory.

Over the years, with social media becoming more and more accessible, the clip has become even more notorious. Moreover, with so many cameras around, such play-acting doesn't go unnoticed as easily, or even if it does in the moment, it is replayed in 15-second reels, bringing enough disrepute to the player.

Dakar Rally Behind Its Lions

Senegal's win over defending champions France on 31 May 2002 remains one of the most unexpected results in FIFA World Cup history. In Dakar, the result triggered a frenzy that blended sporting joy with profound post-colonial symbolism, as the former colony defeated its colonizer on the world stage.

Onlookers reported that the capital was instantly awash in the national colours as soon as the game ended. Fans of all ages ran and danced through the streets, many draped in the Senegalese flag, as the city was serenaded by the deafening roar of car and taxi horns.

The victory even prompted immediate state-level recognition. President Abdoulaye Wade famously joined the celebrations and was seen precariously balanced on the roof of a four-wheel-drive vehicle, holding a football aloft while touring the crowded streets.

He later declared a public holiday to allow the country's 10 million citizens to celebrate properly – schools, offices and even government services were closed to accommodate the nationwide party.

In a lasting tribute, a public square near the Dakar oceanfront was renamed Place des Lions de la Teranga in honour of the team who were nicknamed the Lions of Teranga.

QUIZ

Questions

Kick-Off

1. Why was South Korea's name featured first in the official title of the tournament? Leading to displeasure amongst the Japanese officials, what anomaly did they indulge in as a form of protest for the same?
2. Which country's jersey was deemed ineligible by FIFA because it was sleeveless? Interestingly, they had used it at the 2002 African Nations Cup without any objections.
3. On the day of the final of the 2002 World Cup, which two lowest-ranked teams in the world contested in a game dubbed as the 'The Other Final'?
4. In an unusual anecdote behind one of the tournament's most iconic images, Ronaldo revealed that his young son once mistook him for a teammate. This prompted the striker to adopt his famous 2002 haircut? Who was this teammate.
5. Which country became the first from outside Europe or South America to make it to the semi-finals of the World Cup since, when the USA made the last four?

Extra-Time

6. Defending champions France had a campaign to forget as they bowed out of this edition without a goal scored. Which superstar striker's ejection soured the only point they secured at the tournament, a goalless draw against Uruguay?
7. Which captain and one of the most influential players from his country clashed with manager Mick McCarthy in the lead-up to the tournament and was sent home consequently, thus missing the opportunity to play in his second World Cup?
8. About which player, who ensured Italy's heartbreaking exit from the tournament, did Perugia owner Luciano Gaucci launch a verbal attack, saying: 'That gentleman will never set foot in Perugia again. He was a phenomenon only against Italy. I have no intention of paying a salary to someone who has ruined Italian football.'?
9. The official mascots for the 2002 FIFA World Cup, hosted by South Korea and Japan, were a trio of futuristic, computer-generated creatures called Ato, Kaz and Nik. They were the first World Cup mascots that were not based on animals, people, or objects, and the first to be designed entirely in 3D. What were they collectively called?
10. At the 1974 World Cup, the then federal capital of the host country (West Germany), Bonn, didn't host a single game. This has only been repeated once since – which capital city (not the greater metropolitan area) emulated this in 2002?

Shoot-Out

11. Despite South Korea kicking off the fixture, Turkish striker İlhan Mansız quickly pounced on a defensive error by Hong Myung-bo, setting up which player for what remains the fastest goal ever scored in a World Cup match after just 11 seconds?
12. In the semi-final, which player scored the winning goal against South Korea in Seoul, sending Germany to the final but, after receiving a yellow card in the 71st minute – his second of the knockout stage – was suspended for the final against Brazil?

13. On 6 May 2001, which Togo player, aged just 13 years and 310 days, became the youngest ever to feature in a FIFA World Cup qualifier? He was later even signed by Manchester United but due to work permit issues, never played a game for the English giants.
14. In a unique instance, which father-son duo appeared at this World Cup for two different teams? While the father coached Paraguay, the son represented Italy.
15. Australia's 31–0 victory over American Samoa on 11 April 2001 in the qualifiers remains the world record for the largest winning margin in a senior international football match. Played at the International Sports Stadium in Coffs Harbour, the match also saw which player set an individual world record by scoring 13 goals in a single international game?

Crossword

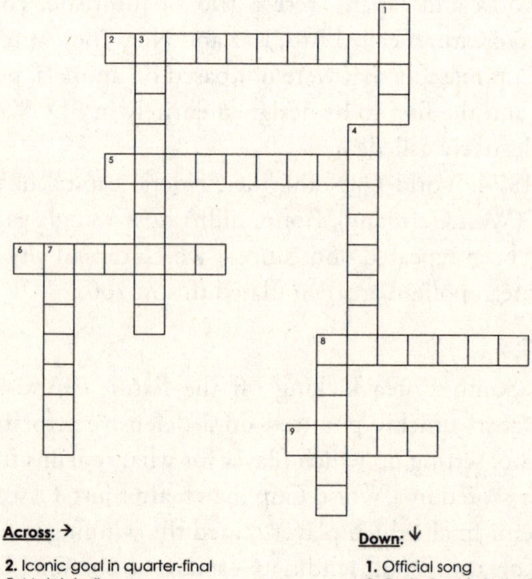

Across: →

2. Iconic goal in quarter-final
5. Match ball
6. Winning manager
8. Only indoor stadium
9. First yellow card

Down: ↓

1. Official song
3. Costly fumble in the final
4. Sent off from the bench
7. Referee of the final
8. Eliminated by Golden Goal

ANSWER KEY

Answers to Questions

1. French spellings were used, and hence 'Corea' appeared before Japan alphabetically; in protest, the Japanese refused to use the entire name of the event, referring to it as the FIFA World Cup 2002 instead of FIFA World Cup 2002 Korea Japan.
2. Cameroon
3. Bhutan and Montserrat
4. Roberto Carlos
5. South Korea
6. Thierry Henry
7. Roy Keane
8. Ahn Jung-hwan
9. Spheriks
10. Tokyo
11. Hakan Şükür
12. Michael Ballack
13. Souleymane Mamam
14. Cesare and Paolo Maldini
15. Archie Thompson

Solution to Crossword

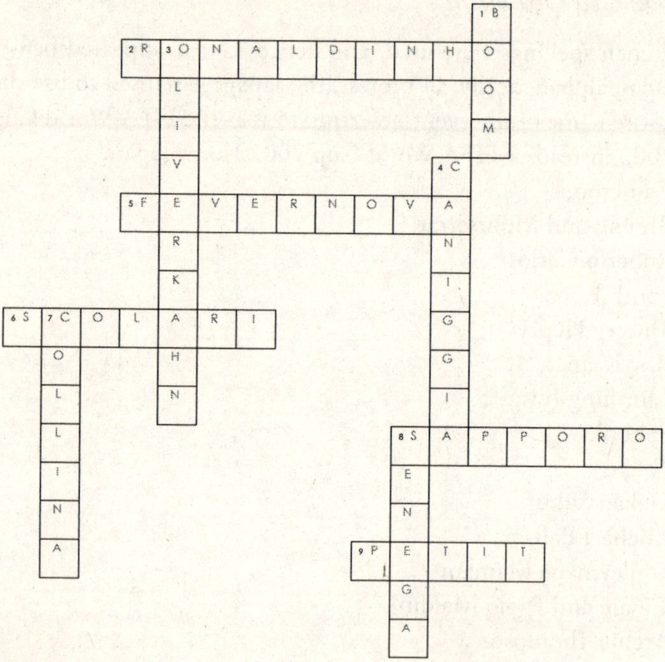

Across: →

2. Iconic goal in quarter-final
5. Match ball
6. Winning manager
8. Only indoor stadium
9. First yellow card

Down: ↓

1. Official song
3. Costly fumble in the final
4. Sent off from the bench
7. Referee of the final
8. Eliminated by Golden Goal

2006, GERMANY

STORIES

Zidane Moment of Indiscretion

The legendary Zinedine Zidane had come out of retirement to lead France on a miraculous run to the final. He was 110 minutes into the last game of his professional life, having already scored a Panenka penalty earlier in the match. It was shaping up to be a fairy-tale ending to a glorious career, but in a moment of uncharacteristic violence, it all changed.

The image of the midfielder's forehead striking the chest of Italian defender Marco Materazzi left the world shocked.

The confrontation occurred during the second half of extra time, with the score deadlocked at 1–1. As the two players jogged back towards midfield, Materazzi was seen tugging at Zidane's jersey. Zidane apparently said, 'If you want my shirt, I will give it to you afterwards.' The Italian fired back with a crude insult regarding Zidane's sister.

What happened next was a lapse in judgement that defied Zidane's usual composure. He stopped, turned and lunged forward, driving his head into Materazzi's chest.

The referee, Horacio Elizondo, did not see the incident. It was only after a frantic consultation with the fourth official, who had seen the replay on a monitor, that the red card was produced. As Zidane walked off the pitch, head bowed, he passed the World Cup Trophy sitting on its plinth. He didn't look at it; he had just erred on the grandest stage of them all, and it just proved again that sports is a great leveller – you could be celebrated as a hero and, minutes later, walk with your head down and see your team helplessly lose a World Cup final.

Italy's Unlikely Hero

In 2001, Fabio Grosso was playing in the fourth division of Italian football, the lowest professional league in the country. Five years later, he stepped up to hand the Azzurri their fourth and so far last World Cup win.

Since his days in Serie C2, he had joined Perugia and then moved to Palermo, but even when he was picked in the World Cup squad, he was seen as an outsider in a squad filled with Champions League winners and global icons.

He really came of age, though, in the dying seconds against Australia. With the match deadlocked at 0–0 and Italy down to 10 men, Grosso surged into the box in the 93rd minute. He drew a foul from Lucas Neill, winning a controversial but decisive penalty. Francesco Totti converted it, but it was Grosso's marauding run that had saved Italy from the precipice of an embarrassing exit.

Then, in the semi-final against the hosts, Germany, as the match drifted towards a penalty shoot-out in the 119th minute, Italy won a corner. The ball found its way to Andrea Pirlo, who played a no-look pass to the edge of the area.

Grosso met the ball first time, curling a magnificent strike into the far corner of the net. His celebration – a frantic, head-shaking sprint – became one of the defining images of the tournament. It was a mirror of Marco Tardelli's iconic 1982 celebration, signalling to an entire nation that the dream was real.

In the final, too, against France, after 120 minutes of gruelling football, the game went to penalties. Italy had lost their last three World Cup shoot-outs (in 1990, 1994, 1998), but Marcello

Lippi, the Italian manager, chose Grosso to take the fifth and final kick. With the weight of a nation on his shoulders, the man who had been relatively unknown until the tournament started, stepped up and buried the ball into the top corner.

Two Icons Make Their World Cup Debut

In 2006, an 18-year-old Lionel Messi and a 21-year-old Cristiano Ronaldo made their World Cup debuts. This was the first of five editions of the tournament that the two greats played in.

While Messi arrived in Germany as a teenager with long, shaggy hair and the weight of a nation comparing him to Diego Maradona already on his shoulders, Ronaldo had already gained quite a reputation as an explosive winger set to dominate world football.

To say that the two of them had contrasting tournaments would be apt – Messi, after sitting out of his team's opening match, made his debut against Serbia and Montenegro, coming on as a substitute in the 74th minute.

His impact was instantaneous; within three minutes, he provided an assist for Hernan Crespo. Ten minutes later, he latched onto a Carlos Tévez pass and slotted home his first World Cup goal. In just 15 minutes of play, he had become the youngest-ever Argentine to play and score in the tournament.

However, in the quarter-final against Germany, manager José Pékerman famously left him on the bench as Argentina was eliminated on penalties.

Ronaldo, on the other hand, was a focal point of Portugal's 'Golden Generation' swan-song tournament.

Donning the number 17 jersey (since Luís Figo still wore 7), his debut against Angola was relatively quiet, but he found his footing in the second match against Iran, where he confidently converted a penalty. Then, in the quarter-final against England, he was vilified by the media and fans after he was caught winking at his bench following the red card shown to his Manchester United teammate, Wayne Rooney.

While the world debated his sportsmanship, Ronaldo proved his steel by scoring the winning penalty in that shoot-out, leading Portugal to their first semi-final in 40 years.

Scribbled Cheat Code

During the 2006 quarter-final between Germany and Argentina in Berlin, the 'Lehmann Note', a crumpled piece of hotel stationery tucked into the German goalkeeper's sock, became the most iconic scrap of paper in World Cup history.

The hosts were deadlocked at 1–1 with an Argentina side that many believed was the best in the world. As the match moved to penalties, German goalkeeper coach Andreas Köpke handed Jens Lehmann a small piece of paper from a notebook provided by the team's hotel. It wasn't a lucky charm; it was a tactical cheat sheet detailing the tendencies of the opposition penalty takers.

What followed was a masterclass in playing mind games – before every Argentine player stepped up to the spot, Lehmann would reach into his right sock, pull out the paper, and study it. This was almost a signal to Argentines that he knew which way they were going to shoot.

The results supported this rather unusual method. For Roberto Ayala's penalty, the note read: 'Wait long, long run-up, right.' Lehmann followed the instructions perfectly, remained centred until the last microsecond, and dived right to make the save. For Maxi Rodríguez, the note simply said 'Left'. Although Rodríguez scored, Lehmann dived the correct way, missing the ball by inches.

The climax of the story, however, relies on a brilliant bluff. When Esteban Cambiasso stepped up for the final, deciding penalty, Lehmann again pulled out the paper and studied it with intense focus. In reality, Cambiasso's name was not on the list. The coaching staff hadn't anticipated him taking a penalty. Yet, the sight of Lehmann checking his notes likely sowed a seed of doubt in Cambiasso's mind. Lehmann guessed left, saved the shot, and sent Germany into the semi-finals.

The note itself became a cultural artefact. In December 2006, it was auctioned for €1 million (US$1.3 million), a staggering sum for a piece of hotel stationery, with the proceeds going to a children's charity.

An Astrology Enthusiast

In the oddest of tales from this tournament, French coach Raymond Domenech reportedly checked birth charts and star signs to determine his squad.

His most famous casualty was Robert Pires – a legend of Arsenal's Invincibles era and a key member of France's 1998 FIFA World Cup–winning team – who, as a Scorpio (born 29 October), found himself inexplicably frozen out of the squad for the 2006 World Cup.

Domenech's rationale was that Scorpios were tough to manage and possessed a personality that would disrupt the harmony of the dressing room.

The manager also feared Leos were too egocentric for defensive duties. He famously remarked that a Leo in defence was a liability because they would try to show off at the back, leading to critical errors.

Additionally, he believed in not playing some players together based on their star signs, which likely cost defenders like Philippe Mexès a spot in his teams too. Mexès, in 2025, spoke about what had transpired almost two decades earlier: 'Aries doesn't play with Scorpio, Scorpio doesn't play with Taurus…' (referring to Domenech's selection policies).

QUIZ

Questions

Kick-Off

1. It is one of those rare moments where the speed of geopolitics outran the logistics of international sports. Which team, during the 2006 World Cup, continued to use the old anthem and flag

of the union they had been part of, despite one republic letting go of the other's confederacy just before the event started?

2. Which German satirical magazine sent packages to FIFA representatives on the night before the vote to elect the hosts for the 2006 edition, with items such as cuckoo clocks and ham sealed inside?
3. In the 2006 World Cup, why were the names of several iconic stadiums temporarily altered? While you are at it, name the stadium in Munich that FIFA rebranded for the tournament, and explain how Munich avoided a similar issue when it hosted the World Cup in 1974. (Similar naming adjustments are taking place in the 2026 edition of the tournament.)
4. Name the quiet spa-town that served as England's base leading up to the tournament. With the team allowed to have their partners stay with them, paparazzi flocked into the camp and focused extensively on WAGs, or 'wives and girlfriends'. Critics believed this hampered the team's performance and thus, in subsequent editions of the World Cup, most managers have opted for locked-down camps.
5. As Australia tried to make it to their first World Cup in 32 years, they had to beat Uruguay in the inter-continental play-off to qualify for the tournament. When the teams remained level after two legs, the tie was decided by a penalty shoot-out; goalkeeper Mark Schwarzer emerged as the hero, stopping two of Uruguay's spot-kicks. But who was the player who converted the final penalty and then ran across the field in what has since become an iconic part of their history in the sport?

Extra-Time

6. Which two teams competed in an ugly Round of 16 fixture that saw Russian referee Valentin Ivanov hand out a total of 20 cards (16 yellow and 4 red)?
7. Leading up to their match against Ivory Coast, over 1,000 Dutch fans were stopped at the gates of the stadium in Stuttgart

for wearing bright orange overalls featuring the logo of the Dutch brewer Bavaria. Since Budweiser was the official FIFA beer sponsor, officials deemed the overalls ambush marketing. What comical sight ensued as a result?

8. Which country's play off against Bahrain was ordered to be replayed by FIFA citing a 'refereeing error'? The team in question had won that game 1–0 but later couldn't win the revised fixture and thus couldn't qualify for the World Cup. Their maiden appearance at the tournament is going to happen in 2026.
9. What break from a World Cup tradition saw hosts Germany take on Costa Rica in the opening game of the tournament?
10. What iconic FIFA World Cup moment is *The Guardian*'s Barry Glendenning describing here?:

    'The goal of the tournament so far and quite possibly the greatest goal that's ever been scored.

    'Ping. _________. Crespo. _________… goal!'

Shoot-Out

11. Which team lost to Ukraine on penalties after a goalless draw, thus becoming the first ever in tournament history to get eliminated without conceding a single goal at an edition?
12. Which two countries provided four head coaches each amongst the 32 participating teams at this tournament? If it helps, one of them had coaches in charge of Brazil, Japan, Portugal and Saudi Arabia, while coaches from the other led Australia, the Netherlands, South Korea and Trinidad and Tobago.
13. In the quarter-final between Argentina and Germany, who became the first and, till then, the only player to be shown a red card after the penalty shoot-out in a World Cup fixture?
14. Zinedine Zidane scored in the final against Italy to become only the fourth player ever, after Vavá, Pelé and Geoff Hurst, to have

cumulatively scored three goals in World Cup finals. Which countryman of his broke this record in 2022?

15. What animal was Goleo VI, the mascot of the 2006 World Cup? It was widely criticized and considered strange given it was not a native German animal, but rather the emblem of historical rivals England and the Netherlands.

Anagrams

Unscramble the following to identify the stadiums that were temporarily renamed for the 2006 World Cup because of sponsorship reasons:

1. AAASPLUNKINGRID
2. ENRAOALA
3. BRAMAMENAZONRECK
4. ENGINEEREDHISTORIAN
5. EDNARAWA

ANSWER KEY

Answers to Questions

1. Serbia and Montenegro
2. *Titanic*
3. To comply with FIFA's rules prohibiting corporate sponsor names, Allianz Arena in Munich was temporarily called FIFA World Cup Stadium Munich for the tournament; the stadium used in 1974 was called Olympiastadion and did not require any renaming, as it was not named after a sponsor.
4. Baden-Baden
5. John Aloisi
6. Portugal and the Netherlands
7. Spectators took over their jumpsuits and watched the game in just their underwear.

8. Uzbekistan
9. Defending champions not playing the first game of the tournament
10. Esteban Cambiasso's iconic 26-move goal
11. Switzerland
12. Brazil and the Netherlands
13. Leandro Cufré
14. Kylian Mbappé
15. Lion

Solutions to Anagrams

1. Signal Iduna Park
2. AOL Arena
3. Commerzbank-Arena
4. RheinEnergieStadion
5. AWD Arena

2010, SOUTH AFRICA

STORIES

A Polarizing Musical Instrument

The vuvuzela was the unexpected, polarizing protagonist of the 2010 FIFA World Cup. The relentless, low-frequency drone of these plastic horns is something billions of people around the world still remember from the tournament.

Standing at roughly 65 centimetres long, the instrument produced a loud, monotonous sound frequently compared to a swarm of angry bees or a stampeding herd of elephants. In the context of South African football, the horn was a symbol of joy and unity, used by fans to scare the opponents and energize their own team, and, for local supporters, the noise was the heartbeat of the stadium.

However, as the tournament progressed, the sound became a source of intense international friction. The primary criticism came from players and broadcasters. Goalkeepers, such as France's Hugo Lloris, complained that it made it impossible to communicate with their defenders. Broadcasters, meanwhile, struggled to mix audio so that commentators could be heard over the background noise. Even viewers at home were affected; television networks were forced to implement sophisticated audio filters to dampen the frequency of the horns, which many found physically draining to listen to for 90 minutes.

Despite calls to ban it, FIFA president Sepp Blatter stood firm in his defence of the instrument and famously tweeted, 'I have always said that Africa has a different rhythm, a different sound… I don't see banning the music traditions of fans in their own country.'

Despite the complaints, thousands of these instruments were still sold daily to international tourists, and vuvuzela apps briefly topped the app store, ringtone and caller-tune charts.

Lampard's Ghost Goal

In the 37th minute of England's 2010 World Cup Round of 16 clash against Germany, Frank Lampard unleashed a volley that seemed to clearly cross the goal line but was still disallowed.

It came at a crucial juncture too – England had just clawed back to 2–1 through a Matthew Upson header when Lampard struck a high, looping shot from the edge of the area. The ball beat German goalkeeper Manuel Neuer, crashed off the underside of the crossbar, and bounced clearly, by nearly a yard, behind the goal line before spinning back into play.

While Lampard and his teammates began to celebrate what appeared to be a 2–2 equalizer, Uruguayan referee Jorge Larrionda and assistant Mauricio Espinosa signalled for play to continue. Television replays immediately confirmed the ball was well over the line, but without technological aid, the officials' live decision stood.

Instead of entering half-time with renewed momentum at 2–2, England remained a goal down and eventually collapsed to a 1–4 defeat as Germany exploited their desperate search for an equalizer in the second half.

The global outcry was immense. The 'ghost goal', as it was referred to, acted as a catalyst for goal-line technology being introduced by the International Football Association Board (IFAB). It was first officially deployed at the 2012 Club World Cup and has since become a staple at all global events.

Kiwis Remain Unbeaten

The most statistically improbable story of the 2010 FIFA World Cup belonged to New Zealand. Despite being the lowest-ranked team in the competition and failing to progress past the group stage, the All Whites finished as the only unbeaten team in the entire tournament.

Entering only their second-ever World Cup, the expectations from Oceania's entry to the event were fairly modest; the squad simply hoped to secure their first-ever tournament point after losing every match in their debut in 1982. Drawn into Group F alongside reigning champions Italy, a strong Paraguay side and Slovakia, they were widely dismissed and were not given much of a chance.

And that seemed to hold just until the 93rd minute of their opening match; it was then that Winston Reid scored a dramatic header to cancel out Slovakia's lead and secure New Zealand's first-ever World Cup point. In the next game, they shocked the world as Shane Smeltz put New Zealand ahead in the seventh minute against Italy. Although the defending champions equalized via a penalty, the All-Whites' disciplined defence, led by captain Ryan Nelsen, held them to a draw.

A gritty scoreless draw in their final match confirmed their undefeated status, though it wasn't enough to leapfrog Slovakia for a spot in the Round of 16.

Their achievement is unique because even the eventual champions, Spain, lost their opening game to Switzerland. While the Kiwis finished third in their group and were eliminated, they famously joined a select group of teams who remained unbeaten through a FIFA World Cup campaign.

North Korea's Foray into Live Television

North Korea had qualified for the World Cup for the first time in over four decades, and the most enduring image of the start of their campaign in 2010 occurred before a ball was even kicked in their opening match against Brazil. As the opening strains of their national anthem filled Ellis Park Stadium, star striker Jong Tae-se burst into uncontrollable, heaving sobs.

For the global audience, it was a sight they hadn't been exposed to – a North Korean exhibiting vulnerability. Jong, who was born in

Japan to a pro-Pyongyang family, later explained that his tears were born of overwhelming pride and the realization of a lifelong dream to represent his country on football's greatest stage. His emotional display set the tone for a gritty performance in which the 105th-ranked North Koreans shocked the world, losing only 2–1 to five-time champions Brazil.

In North Korea, state media typically exerts absolute control over information, usually airing sporting events hours or days after they conclude to ensure they can be edited to fit the regime's narrative. However, buoyed by the competitive performance against Brazil, the government took an unprecedented gamble: they decided to broadcast the second group match against Portugal live and in full across the nation.

Thus, on 21 June 2010, families across North Korea gathered around television sets to watch a game taking place thousands of miles away in real time. It was believed to be the first time a North Korean match played abroad was ever aired live domestically. The move proved to be catastrophic for the state propaganda regime, as after a competitive first half, North Korea's defence collapsed, and Portugal began scoring at will, eventually winning 7–0.

Post full time, it is reported that the commentator briefly acknowledged the defeat before abruptly ending the feed and cutting to unrelated footage of locals praising North Korean leadership. What was supposed to rally national solidarity instead became a rare viewing of national failure for the citizens in Pyongyang.

Wavin' Flag

While Shakira's 'Waka Waka' was the official anthem of the 2010 FIFA World Cup, K'naan's 'Wavin' Flag' became the tournament's most emotionally resonant signature tune. Originally written as a deep, somber reflection on the Somali Civil War, it was transformed into a global celebration of unity through a high-profile partnership with Coca-Cola.

First released in 2009 on K'naan's album *Troubadour*, its original lyrics were far from celebratory, detailing the struggles of refugees, poverty-stricken neighbourhoods/zones and the hope for freedom amidst violence. When the Coca-Cola company selected it as the promotional anthem for their 2010 World Cup campaign, the song underwent a significant 'Celebration Mix' remix; references to settling scores and struggling to eat were replaced with uplifting lines about champions taking the field and rejoicing in the beautiful game.

Approximately 50 drums were added to the mix to create a high-energy, infectious rhythm that reflected the celebratory spirit of South African culture. The song was also adapted into over 20 different bilingual and country-specific versions, featuring artists like David Bisbal (Spanish), Nancy Ajram (Arabic) and Skank (Portuguese).

By the time the tournament ended, the song's chorus, 'When I get older, I will be stronger / They'll call me freedom, just like a waving flag', became an anthem of hope. It topped the charts in 14 countries and has since become one of the most streamed World Cup songs in history.

QUIZ

Questions

Kick-Off

1. Which world leader, instrumental in bringing the tournament to Africa for the first time, emphasized the importance of football by citing his experience of playing the game while he was imprisoned in Robben Island, when he said, '(Football) made us feel alive and triumphant despite the situation we found ourselves in'?
2. In 2010, Spain became the first team ever to win the World Cup after losing their opening game. They also became the first in over three decades to win after losing a game in the group

stage – which was the last country that had managed this, and in which edition?

3. During the second leg of their World Cup qualifying play-off, French captain Thierry Henry twice illegally handled the ball – unseen by the referee – in the lead-up to the decisive goal that sent France through. Which team, affected by the incident, first requested a replay on fairness grounds and was then included as an unprecedented 33rd World Cup entrant?
4. The Orlando Stadium in Soweto, a suburb of Johannesburg, wasn't an official venue, and yet became part of the World Cup legacy a day before the tournament started on 10 June. What event took place here?
5. The Makhonya Royal Trust had suggested a ritual they called a 'truly African' event at each stadium to bless the tournament. Given its absurdity, the idea was abandoned and a compromise was reached for a one-off on 25 May at the Soccer City Stadium. What precisely was their proposal?

Extra-Time

6. Which compatriot did Andrés Iniesta pay homage to after scoring the winner in the final against the Netherlands? The Spanish midfielder had the name of this player, who had passed away the previous year, written on his undershirt.
7. Which striker was famously expelled from the French team by coach Raymond Domenech after a ferocious row during the half-time break of their loss against Mexico?
8. Having received a pass from Elano on the right side of the penalty area, which Brazilian defender, from an extremely tight, almost impossible angle near the goal line, struck the ball with the outside of his right foot and scored an iconic goal? The ball, almost defying the laws of physics, swerved sharply past North Korean goalkeeper Ri Myong-guk and into the far corner of the net.

9. In the last minute of extra-time during their quarter-final, which Ghanaian player's goal-bound header did Luis Suárez deliberately use his hands to block, thus ensuring the African team didn't take a decisive lead?
10. Which occupant of the Sea Life Centre in Oberhausen, Germany, achieved global fame during this tournament with its accurate predictions for outcomes of games?

Shoot-Out

11. The first time two brothers played against each other in a full international FIFA World Cup match occurred on 23 June 2010. Name the two siblings who faced off in a Group D match between Germany and Ghana in Johannesburg.
12. During the 2010 FIFA World Cup, the South African national football team (Bafana Bafana) featured a notable pre-game ritual where players huddled together and placed their hands on which teammate's head?
13. FIFA regulations mandated every team to register three goalkeepers in their 23-member squad. Which team attempted to trick the organizers by enlisting a striker as one of its goalkeepers – their bluff didn't work though as the player was mandated to play as a goalkeeper only if he did indeed take the field at any point.
14. How did a Cameroonian makossa song, 'Zangaléwa', capture the attention of the world during this tournament?
15. The stands in the FNB Stadium were marked by ten black vertical lines. Nine of these were geographically aligned with the other nine stadiums used during the 2010 World Cup. Where did the tenth line aim towards?

Word Search

In total, 13 players were booked in the final of the 2010 World Cup. Search through the puzzle to find their names.

V	N	W	G	P	W	W	O	H	I	D	C	C	B	C	T	L	I
A	Y	Q	I	B	X	V	T	H	N	O	V	A	R	N	H	M	E
N	R	K	M	P	D	A	F	B	I	Y	W	P	O	X	E	D	Q
B	A	F	A	O	A	N	J	E	E	L	O	D	N	T	I	Y	N
O	M	X	T	W	U	D	G	Q	S	N	P	E	C	D	T	C	R
M	O	A	H	R	U	E	B	H	T	H	K	V	K	O	I	D	O
M	S	V	I	X	T	R	M	P	A	W	O	I	H	L	N	E	B
E	T	I	J	R	M	W	L	U	U	Z	U	L	O	K	G	J	B
L	B	M	S	L	M	I	H	Y	S	W	W	A	R	Y	A	O	E
B	G	E	E	J	X	E	I	O	M	C	L	Y	S	D	D	N	N
L	Q	U	N	W	S	L	I	L	C	O	P	A	T	P	W	G	P
A	U	L	G	O	U	P	V	A	N	P	E	R	S	I	E	S	O

Find the following words in the puzzle.
Words are hidden →, ↓, and ↘.

BRONCKHORST
VAN DER WIEL
MATHIJSEN
VAN BOMMEL
VAN PERSIE
CAPDEVILA
HEITINGA
INIESTA
DE JONG
ROBBEN
RAMOS
PUYOL
XAVI

ANSWER KEY

Answers to Questions

1. Nelson Mandela
2. Argentina, 1978
3. Republic of Ireland
4. The FIFA World Cup celebration concert (first such event in tournament history)
5. They recommended a cow being slaughtered at every stadium.
6. Dani Jarque
7. Nicolas Anelka

8. Maicon
9. Dominic Adiyiah
10. Paul the Octopus
11. Jérôme Boateng (Germany) and Kevin-Prince Boateng (Ghana)
12. Steven Pienaar
13. North Korea (player: Kim Myong-won)
14. 'Waka Waka (This Time for Africa)' was sampled on this song.
15. Berlin's Olympic Stadium, which hosted the previous World Cup final in 2006

Solution to Word Search

V	.	.	.	.	.	.	.	.	I	.	.	C	B	.	.	.	.
A	.	.	.	.	.	V	.	.	N	.	.	A	R	.	H	.	.
N	R	.	M	.	.	A	.	.	I	.	.	P	O	.	E	.	.
B	A	.	A	.	.	N	.	.	E	.	.	D	N	.	I	.	.
O	M	X	T	.	.	D	.	.	S	.	.	E	C	.	T	.	R
M	O	A	H	.	.	E	.	.	T	.	.	V	K	.	I	D	O
M	S	V	I	.	.	R	.	P	A	.	.	I	H	.	N	E	B
E	.	I	J	.	.	W	.	U	.	.	.	L	O	.	G	J	B
L	.	.	S	.	.	I	.	Y	.	.	.	A	R	.	A	O	E
.	.	.	E	.	.	E	.	O	.	.	.	.	S	.	.	N	N
.	.	.	N	.	.	L	.	L	.	.	.	.	T	.	.	G	.
.	.	.	.	.	.	.	V	A	N	P	E	R	S	I	E	.	.

Word directions and start points are formatted: (Direction, X, Y)

BRONCKHORST (S,14,1)
VAN DER WIEL (S,7,2)
MATHIJSEN (S,4,3)
VAN BOMMEL (S,1,1)
VAN PERSIE (E,8,12)
CAPDEVILA (S,13,1)
HEITINGA (S,16,2)
INIESTA (S,10,1)
DE JONG (S,17,6)
ROBBEN (S,18,5)
RAMOS (S,2,3)
PUYOL (S,9,7)
XAVI (S,3,5)

2014, BRAZIL

STORIES

Overpromised – Underprepared

The Arena Corinthians, also known as Neo Química Arena stadium, in São Paulo, was scheduled to host the tournament opener between Brazil and Croatia at the 2014 FIFA World Cup. It was supposed to be a great celebration of the sport in a country that arguably loves it like no other, and yet, on the day of the game, on 12 June, it remained famously incomplete.

In November 2013, a giant crane collapsed while hoisting a roof segment at the venue, killing two workers and destroying a portion of the stadium's exterior. Then, in March 2014, a third worker died after falling from a temporary stand. Because of these events, organizers were forced to abandon plans to finish the stadium's roof before the tournament. Many fans in the temporary stands thus remained exposed to the weather as the opening ceremony, and then the game, took place.

Because of the ill-preparedness of the stadium, which was intended to hold 65,000 fans for the opener, the organizers had to reduce its capacity to just over 40,000 for final test events just 11 days before kick-off, because temporary stands had not been fully cleared. There were eventually also reports that even the planned capacity crowd could not be accommodated due to these factors.

In what is a rarity, and pretty unimaginable now, on the day of the opening match, journalists found exposed wires, unfinished interior walls, and a lack of functional Wi-Fi in the media tribune, leading to rampant negative publicity for the event.

Super Fan in Tears

Clóvis Acosta Fernandes, affectionately known as the 'Gaúcho da Copa', was arguably Brazil's most famous superfan. Recognizable by his traditional gaucho hat, thick moustache and a replica of the FIFA World Cup trophy he carried everywhere, he attended over 150 matches across 60 countries, including seven different World Cups starting from 1990. He considered himself the team's 12th man, a title he earned through decades of unwavering devotion.

During the semi-final in Belo Horizonte, as Germany's goals piled up, broadcast cameras captured Clóvis clutching his replica trophy and weeping in the stands. In a match that shattered Brazilian pride, his face became the symbol of sorrow for his entire country. Despite his devastation, Clóvis handed his cherished trophy to a young German fan, asking him to take it to the final.

Sadly, this was the last World Cup game he attended as he passed away on 16 September 2015 at the age of 60 after a nine-year battle with cancer. His death was mourned by football fans worldwide, including the German national football team, which paid tribute to him as a symbol of the beautiful game.

His legacy continues today through his sons, Frank and Gustavo Damasceno. They have attended subsequent World Cups, including those in Russia (2018) and Qatar (2022), carrying their father's famous hat and the same replica trophy to ensure that the memory of their father remains in the stands for every Brazil match.

The Flying Dutchman

In the 43rd minute of the 2014 World Cup opener between the Netherlands and Spain, Robin van Persie produced a moment of athletic brilliance that earned him the nickname 'The Flying Dutchman'. Scored moments before the half-time whistle, this goal spurred not only his team but also brought about the downfall of the then seemingly unbeaten defending champions.

The Dutch move began with a pinpoint 40-yard diagonal pass from defender Daley Blind. As the ball arced through the Salvador air, Van Persie, positioned between defenders Sergio Ramos and Jordi Alba, made a split-second decision. Rather than attempting to control the ball or strike a traditional volley, he launched his entire body into the air. He took flight at the edge of the penalty area, roughly 15–18 yards from the goal, and while suspended horizontally and parallel to the turf, he met the ball with a perfectly guided header. Lifting his head with precision, he looped the ball over a stranded Iker Casillas. The Spanish goalkeeper was rooted to the spot, able only to watch as the ball found the back of the net.

This was a high-stakes rematch of the 2010 World Cup final, and the goal cancelled Xabi Alonso's penalty from earlier. It set the tone for a second-half onslaught in which the Dutch scored four more times, resulting in a 5–1 rout of the defending champions. It marked the largest losing margin ever for a defending World Cup champion.

Van Persie's celebration, as he ran to the sideline to celebrate with coach Louis van Gaal, was thus immortalized and has remained etched in the memories of football fans.

Teething Issues

The Group D match between Uruguay and Italy in Natal was a do-or-die fixture for both teams. In the 79th minute, with the score tied at 0–0, two of their premier players, Luis Suárez and Giorgio Chiellini, clashed.

Television replays showed Suárez had leaned into Chiellini and had gone teeth-first into the defender's shoulder. After the contact, the striker fell to the ground clutching his own teeth as if he were the injured party. Meanwhile, a furious Chiellini pulled down his jersey to show the referee distinct red bite marks. Mexican referee Marco Rodríguez, however, did not see the bite, and therefore, took no action. Just two minutes later, Uruguay's Diego Godín scored the winning goal, securing a 1–0 victory that sent Uruguay to the Round of 16 and eliminated Italy.

Suárez initially claimed he had merely 'lost (his) balance' and hit his face against Chiellini. However, six days after the match, he issued a formal apology on Twitter, admitting that Chiellini had suffered the 'physical result of a bite'.

While the Uruguayan had escaped a red card during the game, FIFA launched an immediate investigation using video evidence. The subsequent ban was unprecedented: he received a four-month ban from all football-related activity, a suspension for nine international matches, and a fine of 1,00,000 Swiss franc. He was also barred from entering any stadium during the ban.

This wasn't his first offence of this nature; in fact, it was the third time Suárez had been sanctioned for biting an opponent, following previous incidents with Ajax in 2010 (against Otman Bakkal) and Liverpool in 2013 (against Branislav Ivanović).

Interestingly, Chiellini eventually expressed admiration for Suárez's malice, stating in his 2020 autobiography that such intensity was part of what made Suárez a great striker. He even called the four-month ban excessive and publicly accepted Suárez's apology.

#ThingsTimHowardCouldSave

During their Round of 16 match against Belgium, American goalkeeper Tim Howard pulled off an iconic performance against a relentless Belgian attack. Over 120 minutes of play, he recorded the most saves in a single World Cup match. Despite his team ultimately losing 1–2, his performance was widely noticed and applauded by everyone, and with social media just beginning to resemble what we know today, the hashtag #ThingsTimHowardCouldSave started trending as the match culminated.

Fans began photoshopping Howard into historical and pop-culture crises, suggesting he could have prevented some of humanity's greatest tragedies and fictional heartbreaks. Some of the funnier ones had him saving the Titanic from the iceberg, preventing the extinction of the dinosaurs, catching Mufasa in *The Lion King*, or saving Ned Stark in *Game of Thrones!*

His Wikipedia page was briefly edited to list him as the US Secretary of Defense, which was acknowledged by President Barack Obama, who joked about making the appointment official!

QUIZ

Questions

Kick-Off

1. Which team did Uruguay beat in the inter-continental qualifier to make it to this tournament? That country, which had never made it to the World Cup before, is finally set to make its debut in 2026.
2. Rather ironically, which member of the England contingent got injured while celebrating Daniel Sturridge's equalizer against Italy and had to be sent back home with a dislocated ankle?
3. Which Ecuadorian player scored 3 goals in the group stage but couldn't help his team qualify for the next round? If it helps, he also scored the opening goal of the 2022 World Cup.
4. What was unique about the hat-trick that Switzerland's Xherdan Shaqiri scored against Honduras in the group stages?
5. In 1978, English Second Division side Sheffield United tried to sign Diego Maradona from Argentinos Juniors. However, the player was too expensive, and instead they turned to which compatriot of his? This player-turned-manager succeeded Maradona as coach of Argentina too and was at the helm as the team made it to the final of the 2014 World Cup.

Extra-Time

6. Which former Chelsea player, who now indulges in long-distance running and had become famous a few years ago for ascending mountains in just shorts, made the all-important assist that Mario Götze scored from in the final?
7. Group D was deemed the Group of Death in this edition. It featured three former World Cup champions, Uruguay, Italy and England, but which country, considered as outsiders, toppled them all to qualify as group winners?
8. In the quarter-final, the Netherlands manager Louis van Gaal orchestrated one of the most audacious tactical manoeuvers in tournament history by substituting goalkeeper Jasper Cillessen just seconds before the final whistle of extra time. Who was brought in as a replacement and helped the Dutch qualify for the next round?
9. Tim Howard set a World Cup record for the most saves in a single match during the USA's Round of 16 tie against Belgium. How many saves did he make?
10. On 15 June 2014, in a Group E match at the Estádio Beira-Rio, French striker Karim Benzema struck a powerful volley in the 48th minute, which hit the inside of the far post, rebounded across the goalmouth, and struck Honduras goalkeeper Noel Valladares. What decision followed next, marking a first in World Cup history?

Shoot-Out

11. Brazilian playmaker Neymar's tournament ended in the quarter-finals with a fractured vertebra. Who was the Colombian player whose challenge caused the injury?
12. In a statement issued on 13 May 2014, which airline announced that it would replace the liveries on eight aircraft to mark the upcoming FIFA World Cup in Brazil? At the time, the company noted that it was the first instance in its 60-year history that

the airline had removed its name from the fuselage of certain aircraft in its fleet.

13. During the Group B match between Spain and Chile, around 100 Chilean supporters who had gathered outside Maracanã Stadium forced their way inside and caused damage to which specific area of the stadium? Earlier, roughly 20 Argentine fans had carried out a similar breach during Argentina's Group F match against Bosnia and Herzegovina at the same stadium.
14. Which player, who had replaced Sami Khedira in the German team in the final, received a blow to the head and had to be substituted in the 31st minute? So disoriented and confused was he that he reportedly asked the referee, Nicola Rizzoli, whether the match he was playing in was the World Cup final.
15. Describe the image that Chinese photographer Bao Tailiang of the *Chengdu Economic Daily* took after the final that won the Sports Singles award at the 2015 World Press Photo awards.

Connect

Group the 16 words into four groups of four. Each group shares a common connection. Each word belongs to one group only.

MARCELO	KLOSE	DAR UM JEITO	KOLAŠINAC
MANAUS	KROOS	VALLADARES	MÜLLER
NATAL	FULECO	SALVADOR	BRAZUCA
WE ARE ONE	KHEDIRA	FORTALEZA	YOBO

ANSWER KEY

Answers to Questions

1. Jordan
2. England's physiotherapist, Gary Lewin

3. Enner Valencia
4. It was the first entirely left-footed hat-trick in World Cup history.
5. Alejandro Sabella
6. André Schürrle
7. Costa Rica
8. Tim Krul
9. Sixteen
10. The first goal awarded using goal-line technology at the World Cup
11. Juan Zúñiga
12. Lufthansa; it called these aircrafts 'Fanhansa'
13. Media centre
14. Christoph Kramer
15. Lionel Messi staring at the World Cup trophy in the photograph titled *The Final Game*

Solution to Connect

MARCELO	KOLAŠINAC	YOBO	VALLADARES	*Own-goalscorers*
MÜLLER	KLOSE	KHEDIRA	KROOS	*Scorers in Germany's 7–1 semi-final victory*
MANAUS	NATAL	FORTALEZA	SALVADOR	*Venues*
FULECO	BRAZUCA	'WE ARE ONE'	'DAR UM JEITO'	*Tournament identity*

2018, RUSSIA

STORIES

One ID, Multiple Benefits

As travel and visa regulations have become increasingly stringent, the FIFA Fan ID for the 2018 FIFA World Cup in Russia, a mandatory personalized spectator card, became a lifesaver for football fans across the world.

It allowed foreign spectators to enter and exit Russia multiple times without a visa by presenting their Fan ID and a valid passport. This benefit was announced to be valid from 10 days before the first match until 10 days after the final.

Holders were also entitled to free travel on special trains connecting the 11 host cities and on local public transport (including the metro, buses, and trams) in those cities on match days, a massive help given the vastness of Russia (the maximum distance between two stadiums was almost 2,500 kilometres!).

For games as well, along with a valid match ticket, the Fan ID was a required document for all spectators, including children, to enter the World Cup stadiums, thus helping authorities identify attendees and prevent known troublemakers from entering the stadiums.

The interesting thing was that, despite the Indian national team not participating, over 4,500 Indian fans purchased tickets and travelled for the tournament, placing India among the top 10 countries for ticket demand during certain sales phases.

This system was a huge success – so much so that the visa-free entry for Fan ID holders was extended through the end of 2018 by the Russian government to encourage further tourism.

Coreano, Hermano, Ya Eres Mexicano!

On 27 June 2018, Mexico was on the verge of being eliminated from the World Cup. After defeating Germany and South Korea in the first two games, the North American team suffered a 3–0 loss against Sweden in their final group match. This loss meant they no longer controlled their own destiny; their only hope for qualification hinged on South Korea either winning or drawing against the defending World Cup champions, Germany.

In a stunning upset, South Korea scored two stoppage-time goals to defeat Germany 2–0, a result that sent the champions home and miraculously secured Mexico's spot in the Round of 16.

What followed next was incredible, to say the least! Hundreds of fans flocked to the South Korean embassy in Mexico City, celebrating the ouster of Germany with the embassy staff. Consul General Byoung-jin Han wasn't spared either, as images of him being hoisted onto the shoulders of the crowd went viral soon after. Fans chanted, '*¡Coreano, hermano, ya eres mexicano*!' ('Korean, brother, you are now Mexican!'). Videos online that were widely shared of fans offering tequila to embassy officials and making them wear Mexico jerseys were extremely wholesome, a reminder of sport's power to unite people across countries and cultures.

And the celebrations didn't stop there either – local radio stations in Mexico City began playing Korean music in honour of the win. The country's national airline, Aeroméxico, announced a 20 per cent discount on flights to South Korea!

For months after the win, Mexico arguably remained the most hospitable country to visit as a South Korean!

Belgium Pull a Houdini

Japan has been incredibly consistent at the World Cups since it hosted the 2002 FIFA World Cup, qualifying for each edition and making it out of the group stages four times. In 2018, though, they came closest to becoming only the third Asian team ever to make it to the quarter-finals.

Against Belgium, two quick-fire goals early in the second half from Genki Haraguchi and Takashi Inui left the world stunned. The turning point, however, arrived in the 65th minute when the Red Devils' manager, Roberto Martínez, made a double substitution: replacing Dries Mertens and Yannick Carrasco with Marouane Fellaini and Nacer Chadli.

The game shifted immediately. Belgium abandoned intricate build-ups for an aerial assault, exploiting their height advantage. In the 69th minute, a looping, somewhat fortuitous header from Jan Vertonghen cut the deficit. Five minutes later, the towering Fellaini hammered home a cross from Eden Hazard, levelling the score and shattering Japan's momentum.

And then, in the final seconds of stoppage time, the turnaround was complete. Japan, refusing to settle for extra time, committed men forward for a corner. Thibaut Courtois gathered the ball and instantly triggered a counter-attack, rolling it to Kevin De Bruyne, who surged through the heart of the pitch. The Manchester City star found Thomas Meunier on the wing, whose low cross was brilliantly dummied by Romelu Lukaku, allowing an unmarked Nacer Chadli to tap in the winner at 90 + 4.

This was the first time a team had recovered from a two-goal deficit in a World Cup knockout game since West Germany did so against England in 1970, and although they couldn't make it to the final, Belgium's golden generation again showed its mettle by dispatching the mighty Brazil in the next round.

As for Japan, that last-eight spot still eludes them.

Mbappé Shines

At the age of just 19, French teenager Kylian Mbappé took the world by storm in this edition. While the goal in the final against Croatia was his crowning achievement, his performance against Argentina in the Round of 16 is widely regarded as his breakout masterpiece. Beyond his 2 goals in that match, he won a critical penalty for France after a sensational 70-yard dash that overwhelmed the Argentine defence. He finished the tournament as the joint second-highest goalscorer, directly contributing to France's record haul of 14 goals at the tournament.

Some of the highlights of his tournament were:

- Youngest goalscorer for France at the World Cup: He achieved this against Peru in the group stage.
- Youngest to score a brace since 1958: In the Round of 16 clash against Argentina, he became the first teenager to score twice in a single World Cup match since Pelé did so in 1958.
- Second youngest scorer in a World Cup final: His goal in the final against Croatia made him only the second teenager in history to score in a World Cup final, again following in Pelé's footsteps.

He was the undisputed recipient of the FIFA World Cup Best Young Player Award, and thus became the second Frenchman, after teammate Paul Pogba, to receive the award.

Neymar Rolls

During this tournament, Brazilian superstar Neymar became the subject of global trolling on social media due to his diving and almost theatrical overreactions to fouls. A widely cited study by Swiss broadcaster RTS calculated that he spent a total of 13 minutes, 50 seconds on the ground during Brazil's first four matches. Over five minutes of this occurred during the Round of 16 match against Mexico alone!

Critics and fans mocked his habit of rolling excessively on the pitch, leading to the creation of the #NeymarChallenge, where people around the world recorded themselves falling and rolling at the sound of his name.

This viral trend saw fans, schoolchildren and even tennis player Jonas Björkman at Wimbledon mocking his antics by dramatically collapsing and rolling. Major brands joined the mockery; KFC South Africa released an advertisement featuring a player rolling out of a stadium and through a city to reach one of their outlets.

People joked that Neymar should receive an Academy Award for his acting skills, particularly after an incident against Mexico where he writhed in pain after his ankle was stepped on.

Initially defensive, Neymar later acknowledged the criticism through a mix of humour and sincerity, posting a video on Instagram participating in his own challenge with a group of children, jokingly coaching them on how to dive for a free-kick.

Later, in a Gillette ad titled 'A New Man Every Day', he admitted, 'You may think I exaggerate. And sometimes I do exaggerate. But the truth is I suffer on the pitch.'

To be fair to him, that part of his statement did hold substance, as he was indeed the most fouled player in the tournament (targeted 23 times in four games), but that doesn't change the fact that his reactions were definitely over the top!

QUIZ

Questions

Kick-Off

1. In the 2018 edition, which Croatian became the first player in history to score both a goal and an own goal in a World Cup final?
2. Which African nation became the first ever team to be eliminated from the World Cup via the Fair Play rule (fewer yellow cards)?

3. At 45 years and 161 days old, which Egyptian goalkeeper became the oldest player to ever play in a World Cup? In his final match against Saudi Arabia, he also saved a penalty from Fahad Al-Muwallad to cement his place in history.
4. After his teammate Adnan Januzaj scored a spectacular curling goal, which Belgian player picked up the ball and attempted to boot it back into the net in celebration, and instead, the ball ricocheted off the woodwork and struck him squarely in the face? When it became a viral meme, he tweeted, 'Ahahha I knew I would be f*cked the minute I come to my mentions. Why am I so stupid bro? Shit hurts.'
5. Which former captain of Senegal led the team to qualification for Russia, overcoming Madagascar over two legs and winning a group that featured Burkina Faso, Cape Verde and South Africa?

Extra-Time

6. Which goalkeeper's save on Fedor Smolov's penalty in the quarter-final made him only the third goalkeeper in history to save four penalties in World Cup shoot-outs? (He had saved three against Denmark in the Round of 16 shoot-out). Sergio Goycochea (Argentina) and Harald Schumacher (Germany) are the other two goalkeepers in that list.
7. Name the two Swiss players who celebrated by making a nationalist gesture honouring their Albanian heritage during Switzerland's 2–1 victory over Serbia. The celebration involved placing their open hands together with their thumbs locked and fingers spread, forming the double-headed eagle seen on Albania's national flag.
8. The inclusion of which host city made this the only World Cup to be hosted across two continents?
9. Which stadium earned the nickname 'Graveyard of Champions' during this tournament as it saw the eliminations of three major football powers: Germany (defending champion, group stage),

Argentina (2014 finalist, Round of 16) and Brazil (five-time champion, quarter-final)?

10. Where was the official ball with which this edition of the World Cup was kicked off between 21 May and 3 June 2018?

Shoot-Out

11. Name the Icelandic goalkeeper who worked as a film director and only went full time in football a few years before the tournament. Before leaving for Russia, he even directed his team's high-energy World Cup commercial for Coca-Cola, and later saved Lionel Messi's spot kick in a historic 1–1 draw for the tiny island nation in their opener.
12. Despite suffering a heartbreaking loss, fans of which side stayed behind for hours to clean the entire stadium section, picking up every piece of litter, thus immediately going viral on social media? Back in the locker room, the distraught players did the same, leaving their dressing room spotless with a note that simply said 'Thank you' in Russian.
13. Name the head of state who iconically sported her team's jersey at the tournament and braved the torrential rain during the presentation ceremony to congratulate her players, earning her the nickname 'The Mother of the Team' on social media?
14. Entering the tournament as the lowest-ranked team, host Russia struggled to hold possession against which powerhouse, completing just 284 passes compared to their opponents 1,137, and yet still managing to defeat them to reach the quarter-final?
15. The match ball burst twice during France's victory over Australia and again in Uruguay's game with Saudi Arabia. In the first incident, Australia centre-back Trent Sainsbury punctured the ball following the challenge on Lucas Hernández. These were just few of the issues that cropped up at the event due to the ball – what was the name of this official match ball created by Adidas for the event?

Crossword

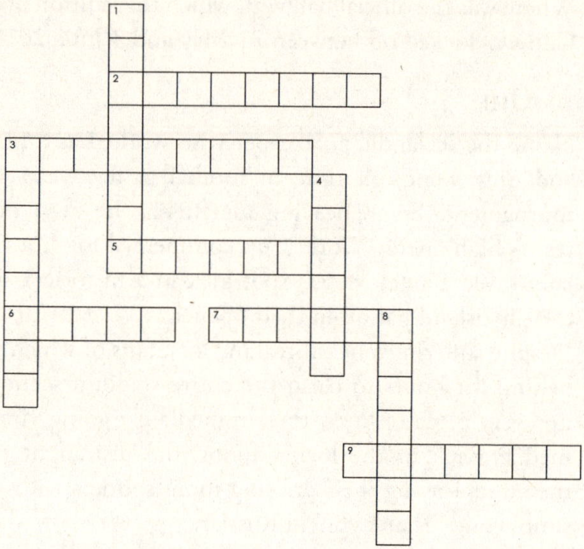

<u>Across</u>: →

2. Mascot
3. Swedish defended who made All Star XI
5. Least populous country at World Cup
6. Only Egyptian to find the net
7. Official sticker maker
9. Defending champions eliminated early

<u>Down</u>: ↓

1. Stadium which hosted the final
3. First goal of the tournament
4. Golden Ball winner
8. Kosovo-Albanian singer of official song

ANSWER KEY

Answers to Questions

1. Mario Mandžukić
2. Senegal
3. Essam El-Hadary
4. Michy Batshuayi
5. Aliou Cissé

6. Danijel Subašić
7. Xherdan Shaqiri and Granit Xhaka
8. Yekaterinburg
9. Kazan Arena
10. Space (International Space Station)
11. Hannes Þór Halldórsson
12. Japan
13. Kolinda Grabar-Kitarović (Croatia's President)
14. Spain
15. Telstar 18

Solution to Crossword

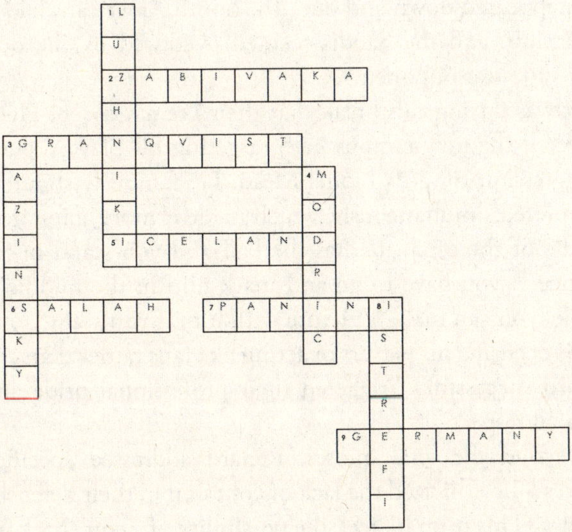

Across: →

2. Mascot
3. Swedish defended who made All Star XI
5. Least populous country at World Cup
6. Only Egyptian to find the net
7. Official sticker maker
9. Defending champions eliminated early

Down: ↓

1. Stadium which hosted the final
3. First goal of the tournament
4. Golden Ball winner
8. Kosovo-Albanian singer of official song

2022, QATAR

STORIES

Renard's Speech Inspires Saudi to Historic Win

In their opening fixture, Saudi Arabia entered the half-time break at Lusail Stadium trailing against Argentina after Lionel Messi opened the scoring from the penalty spot. While the scoreline was close, the team appeared down and out. The South Americans had dominated possession, and the Saudis seemed overawed by the occasion and their superstar opponents.

It was during this break that their French coach, Hervé Renard, delivered the now-famous barb targeting his players' perceived lack of aggression towards Lionel Messi. He famously shouted (and was interpreted simultaneously, which made it more epic): 'Messi, in the middle of the pitch, he has the ball and you stand in front of the defence… you have to go and mark him in the middle! Take your phone, you can make a picture with him if you want!'

By accusing his players of acting like fans rather than competitors, Renard successfully triggered their professional pride and sense of national respect.

Beyond the viral quotes, Renard addressed specific technical failures – he criticized the lack of cohesion in their defensive pressure and urged his team to 'feel' the possibility of a comeback, noting that Argentina was playing relaxed and that they could achieve something special if they simply believed in themselves. He also reminded them of the 35 million people at home in Saudi Arabia waiting for something new.

The result was instantaneous and remarkable to watch as Saudi Arabia seemed a transformed outfit in the second half – first, in the 48th minute, Saleh Al-Shehri equalized, and then just five minutes later, their talismanic midfielder, Salem Al-Dawsari scored a spectacular winning goal to give them the lead.

Over the next 40 minutes, Saudi Arabian defenders played out of their skin to hold on to the lead and thus end Argentina's 36-game unbeaten run, cementing Renard's place in World Cup lore.

Richarlison's Wonder Strike

Brazil was already leading 1–0 in their opening game against Serbia when, in the 73rd minute, after receiving a cross from Vinícius Júnior, Richarlison used his first touch to flick the ball into the air, perfectly positioning it for an unconventional strike. With his back to the goal, he launched himself into a spectacular bicycle kick, connecting cleanly with his right foot to send the ball past the 6 foot 8 inch Serbian goalkeeper into the bottom corner.

The goal was so spectacular that it was later officially named the Hyundai Goal of the Tournament, following a public poll where it beat out other world-class efforts from Kylian Mbappé and Enzo Fernández.

The strike's impact extended far beyond the pitch. In fact, it triggered an immediate and unprecedented surge in Richarlison's digital presence: Within just a few hours of the final whistle, Richarlison gained approximately 4 million new followers on Instagram. This number continued to climb, reportedly exceeding 7 million new followers by the end of the group stage.

Clips of the goal dominated social media platforms too, with fans worldwide attempting to recreate the seemingly impossible physics of the strike.

His pigeon celebration also added to the goal's popularity – the striker got all his teammates and even coach Tite, to join in, and it immediately became quite the sight for fans of the beautiful game. Brazil had come to the World Cup again playing football in the most beautiful and almost surreal manner, and until their exit in the quarter-finals against Croatia, Richarlison's strike set the tone for a fortnight of exceptional showmanship from the Seleção.

Hosts Qatar Disappoint on the Pitch

Entering the tournament as the reigning 2019 AFC Asian Cup champions and ranked 50th in the world, expectations were high for a competitive showing from host Qatar. However, the team struggled with the intensity and tactical discipline required at the World Cup level. The Middle Eastern country managed only 1 goal throughout the entire tournament while conceding 7. It was the statistically worst showing by a host nation in the tournament's 92-year history and marked the end of the tenure of their long-time coach, Félix Sánchez.

It all started to go wrong for them in what was a rescheduled tournament opener. Facing Ecuador, Qatar became the first host nation ever to lose its inaugural game, falling 2–0 on 20 November. Then, in the next game, they lost 3–1 to Senegal, thus becoming the first host nation to be mathematically eliminated from the tournament after just two games. The final nail in their disastrous campaign was a 2–0 loss to the Netherlands. They thus became the first host to finish the group stage with zero points and the first to finish last overall (32nd place) in the tournament rankings.

While many felt they didn't belong to the global stage, that wasn't true. They had come into the tournament having played brilliantly at the continental level, and some of their players also shining in club competitions. In fact, striker Almoez Ali became the first footballer ever to be the highest goalscorer in two different continental competitions (the AFC Asian Cup and the

CONCACAF Gold Cup). And yet, when it mattered the most, with the whole world watching, they came up short – perhaps they will redeem themselves in 2026, but the ghosts from four years before will continue to haunt them.

Korean Miracle at Al Rayyan

Entering their final Group H match against Portugal, the odds were stacked against South Korea qualifying for the next stage. With only one point from their first two games and their talismanic captain, Son Heung-min, suffering a facial fracture, they seemed down and out. But that day, they decided to not give up!

At the Education City Stadium in Al Rayyan, the Taeguk Warriors (nickname of their national team) not only needed to defeat a star-studded Portuguese side that had already won its first two matches. But they also required a specific set of circumstances to unfold in the concurrent match between Uruguay and Ghana. The challenge became even steeper when Portugal took an early lead in the 5th minute through Ricardo Horta. South Korea were staring at elimination, but they didn't give up.

In the 27th minute, Kim Young-gwon capitalized on a deflected corner to equalize, injecting a surge of belief into the squad. And then, in the 91st minute, following a cleared Portuguese corner, Son Heung-min embarked on a desperate, lung-bursting sprint from his own half. As he approached the penalty area, he was surrounded by three defenders. With remarkable composure, he paused and waited for the perfect overlapping run from substitute Hwang Hee-chan. Son threaded a nutmeg pass, allowing Hwang to slot the ball into the bottom corner for a 2–1 lead.

They had done their bit, but qualification still hung in the balance as the Uruguay vs Ghana match was still in its final minutes of stoppage time. The South Korean players gathered in a tight circle in the centre of the pitch, huddled around mobile phones. They were watching a live stream of their rivals' match, knowing that a single goal from Uruguay would end their dream. For nearly ten minutes, the stadium held its breath. When that match finally ended 2–0 to Uruguay, the Korean players erupted in tears of joy.

The margin of victory was historically slim. South Korea and Uruguay finished tied on points (4) and goal difference (0). The Koreans advanced solely on the third tie-breaker: goals scored. They had netted four goals in the group stage to Uruguay's two.

This Miracle of Al Rayyan was complete as the Koreans made it through to their first appearance in the knockout stages of the World Cup in 12 years!

A Final for the Ages

The 2022 FIFA World Cup final, contested between Argentina and France on 18 December 2022, is arguably the greatest World Cup final ever. Both teams were vying for their third title, and for around three hours, the Lusail Stadium became a theatre of the most incredible drama ever witnessed in a sporting enclosure.

The match was rather one-sided until the 80th minute. Lionel Messi opened the scoring with a coolly dispatched penalty in the 23rd minute, becoming the first player to score in every stage of the competition. Then Ángel Di María doubled the lead in the 36th minute following a breathtaking counter-attack that involved five one-touch passes. At half-time, France looked broken, having failed to register a single shot on goal.

However, momentum changed swiftly. In the 80th minute, with the South Americans seemingly coasting to victory, Kylian Mbappé single-handedly altered the game. Within a staggering 97 seconds, he converted a penalty and struck a magnificent falling volley to equalize at 2–2. The stadium, previously a sea of sky blue and white, fell into a stunned silence as the game was forced beyond 90 minutes.

Extra time intensified the drama – in the 108th minute, Messi secured his destiny by bundling home a rebound to make it 3–2. Yet, France refused to give up. In the 118th minute, Mbappé earned another penalty and converted it to become only the second man to score a hat-trick in a World Cup final. The final moments of extra time featured the tournament's most pivotal defensive play – Emiliano Martínez's miraculous spread-eagle save against Randal Kolo Muani, a stop that preserved Argentina's survival.

The resulting penalty shoot-out was a showcase of mental fortitude. Martínez solidified his status as a national hero by saving Kingsley Coman's effort and unnerving Aurélien Tchouaméni into a miss. Argentina, meanwhile, were clinical; Gonzalo Montiel stepped up to score the winning penalty, securing a 4–2 shoot-out victory, and ending a 36-year drought at the World Cup. Cameras zoomed in to Messi collapsing on the centre line as his teammates rushed to celebrate with their legendary leader – he had finally won a World Cup, and it had been done in the most remarkable manner!

QUIZ

Questions

Kick-Off

1. The hosts had a forgettable debut at the tournament, as they lost all games. Which player scored their only goal, and so far the only goal for the hosts at the World Cup?
2. Costa Rica did not have a shot in their 7–0 defeat to Spain. It was the first time in 32 years that a team had gone a whole World Cup game without a shot – which team had done the same at Italia '90?
3. Manager Tite used his entire 26-member squad at the tournament, making Brazil the only team to do so. Who was their third-choice goalkeeper, who was substituted on

for the last 10 minutes of their Round of 16 game against South Korea?

4. While AC Milan, Barcelona, Benfica, Juventus, PSG and Tottenham had two players each, which club had three players starting in the 2022 World Cup final? (The players were: Nahuel Molina and Rodrigo De Paul for Argentina and Antoine Griezmann for France.)
5. Which Brazilian did Kylian Mbappé emulate by becoming the first player to score in two consecutive World Cup finals?

Extra-Time

6. Iranian goalkeeper Alireza Beiranvand had to be substituted in his country's opening match against England, with Hossein Hosseini coming on as his replacement. What was this the first instance of in World Cup history?
7. Italy became the fourth team to miss qualification for the upcoming World Cup despite having won the previous UEFA European Championship. If Czechoslovakia in 1978 and Denmark in 1994 were the first such instances, which was the last team to have met this fate in 2006?
8. How would you connect the three referees who officiated the following matches?
   - UEFA Super Cup 2019 between Liverpool and Chelsea
   - Liga MX Apertura 2020 final between León and Pumas
   - Copa Sudamericana 2020 game between Peñarol and Vélez Sarsfield
9. How would you connect the FIFA Puskás Award–winning goal from 2025 with the last time the ball ended up in the back of the net at the 2022 World Cup?
10. Which Japanese player scored the winner against Spain, a goal that was heavily investigated by video assistant referee (VAR) for potentially going out of play? The dispute was ultimately settled when the Associated Press released an iconic bird's-eye image of the ball after the match.

Shoot-Out

11. Cristiano Ronaldo scored a penalty against Ghana to become the first man to score in five World Cups. Which Canadian, however, had achieved the same distinction earlier in Women's World Cups?
12. The demountable stadium used at this World Cup was designed by a Spanish firm and originally called Ras Abu Aboud Stadium. When it was renamed Stadium 974, two reasons were provided – if the first was that 974 containers were used to make it, what was the other rather obvious reference behind the name?
13. The quarter-final match between Argentina and the Netherlands has often been dubbed as the Battle of Lusail – ill-tempered and volatile was also marred by a tragic incident. Which famous American sportswriter collapsed in the press box near the end of the match and died?
14. In their semi-final against Morocco, which French player scored a goal just 44 seconds after being brought in as a substitute?
15. France were curiously allowed seven substitutions in the final. Which player had suffered a head injury in the 94th minute, thus making his replacement fall under FIFA's concussion protocol, which allows a player at risk of concussion to be substituted without taking into account either the substitution limit for number of players or the substitution window?

Anagrams

Unscramble the following anagrams to name five venues used at the 2022 World Cup

1. OTITICUNDECAY
2. HAAMATLUM
3. BOLAJUAN
4. HANDLEIAMBI
5. AFTONKATHERINALILIAN

ANSWER KEY

Answers to Questions

1. Mohammed Muntari
2. Costa Rica (even then)
3. Weverton
4. Atlético Madrid
5. Vavá
6. First concussion substitute during a World Cup game
7. Greece
8. They formed the first all-women officiating cast at a FIFA men's World Cup match (Germany vs Costa Rica, 2022) (Stéphanie Frappart, Karen Díaz Medina and Neuza Inês Back).
9. Montiel (Santiago Montiel won the FIFA Puskás Award in 2025, while his cousin Gonzalo Montiel scored the winning penalty at the 2022 World Cup final.)
10. Ao Tanaka
11. Christine Sinclair
12. Qatar's international dialling code (974)
13. Grant Wahl
14. Randal Kolo Muani
15. Adrien Rabiot

Solutions to Anagrams

1. Education City
2. Al Thumama
3. Al Janoub
4. Ahmad bin Ali
5. Khalifa International

Tango España: The official match ball

Naranjito: The official mascot

A mural depicting Paolo Rossi celebrating Italy's victory in the 1982 World Cup

Azteca: The official match ball

Pique: The official mascot

A mural depicting the Maradona celebrating the 1986 World Cup win

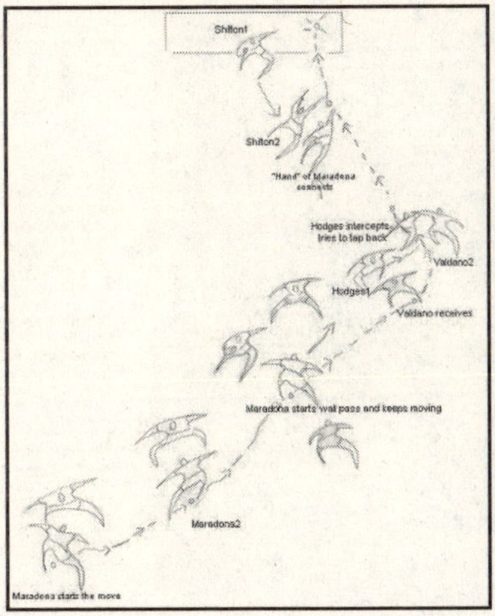

'Hand of God' detailed

Denmark's Jesper Olsen

Stamps commemorating Argentina's 1986 World Cup win and Maradona

Etrusco Unico: The official match ball

Sponsor Mars was prominent at Italia 1990

The Fiat Panda Italia'90 became a cult car

Questra: The official match ball

A Coca-Cola can featuring
Striker, the official mascot

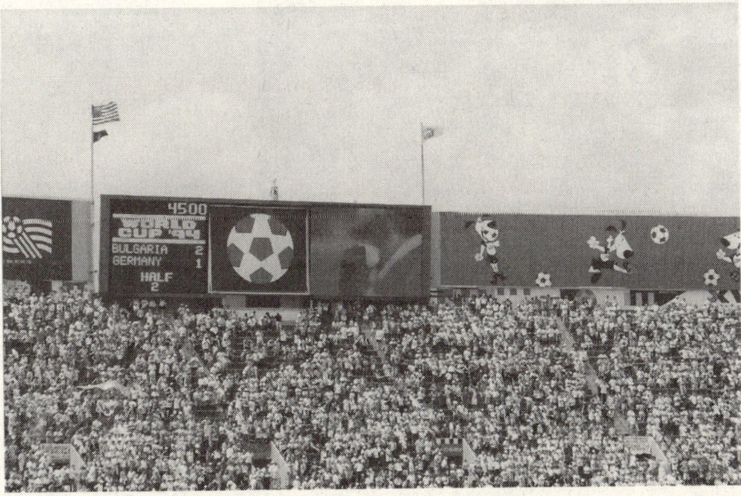

Bulgaria eliminated Germany at the quarter-final

Tartan Army of Scotland

Tricolore: The official match ball

Japan wins in Johor Bahru to qualify for the World Cup

A stuff toy depicting Footix, the official mascot of 1998, displayed in a museum

A view of the Suwon World Cup Stadium

Fevernova: The official match ball

Seoul Plaza filled to the brim

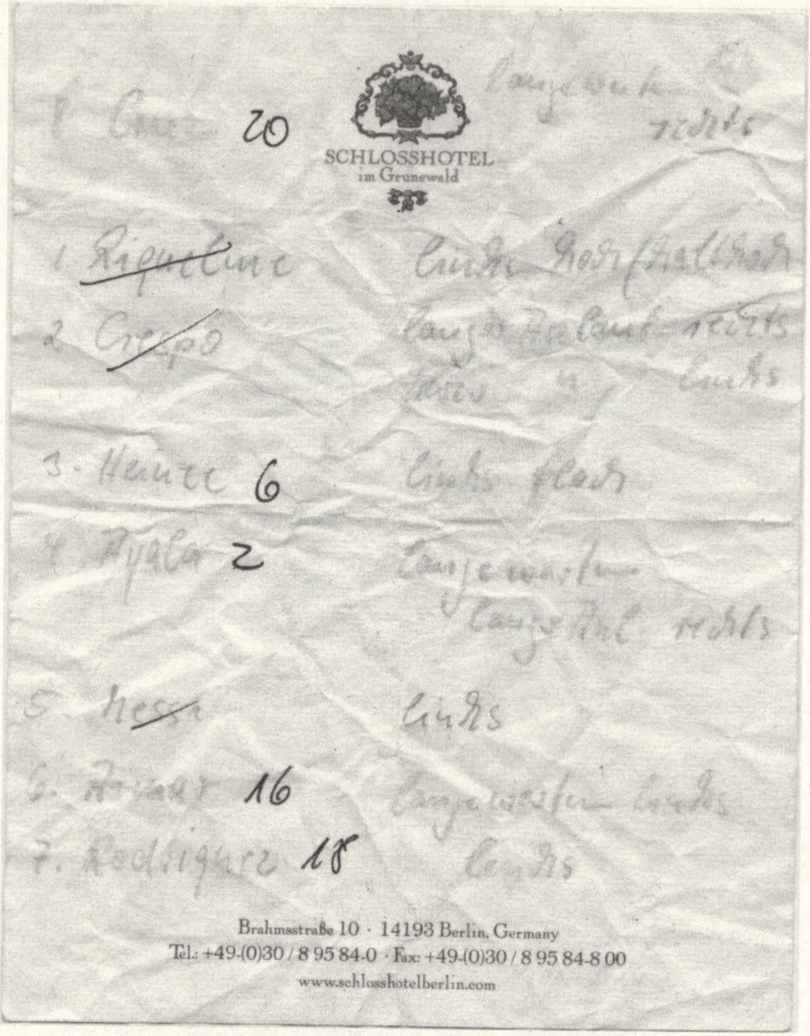

The 'cheat sheet' used by Jens Lehmann against Argentina in the quarter-final penalty shoot-out

The French pennant from the World Cup final

Italy faced off France in the final

Spain coach Vicente del Bosque with the World Cup

Vuvuzelas became a talking point at the tournament

Jabulani: The official match ball

Bastian Schweinsteiger with the World Cup trophy

Brazuca: The official match ball

Clovis Fernandes:
The Brazilian superfan

2014

Germany lifts the FIFA World Cup trophy

A moment from the opening ceremony

Messi playing against Germany in the 2014 final

Mbappé winning the Silver Ball

Telstar 18: The official match ball

France lifts the trophy in Russia

Zabivaka: The official mascot

A sample Fan ID: Russia World Cup's multi-purpose visa

Mbappé celebrates
his goal

Argentina and Mexico ahead of their match
at Lusail Stadium

Argentina fans celebrating at Obelisco, Buenos Aires

The President of FIFA with the 2018
and 2022 host country leaders

Al Rihla: The official
match ball

Messi finally lifts the FIFA World Cup Trophy

2022

IMAGE COPYRIGHT INFORMATION

Note: CCA-SA refers to the Creative Commons Attribution–Share Alike Wikimedia Commons/International Wikimedia Commons licences; Public Domain/PD: All public domain photographs have been sourced from: Wikimedia Commons/Public Domain.

Licences: https://en.wikipedia.org/wiki/en:Creative_Commons;
https://creativecommons.org/licenses/by/2.0/deed.en
https://creativecommons.org/licenses/by-sa/3.0/deed.en; https://creativecommons.org/licenses/by-sa/4.0/deed.en;
https://en.wikipedia.org/wiki/Public_domain;
https://creativecommons.org/licenses/by/4.0/deed.en
https://creativecommons.org/licenses/by-sa/3.0/de/deed.en
https://creativecommons.org/publicdomain/zero/1.0/deed.en
https://en.wikipedia.org/wiki/Fair_use
https://en.wikipedia.org/wiki/GNU_Free_Documentation_License
https://creativecommons.org/licenses/by/3.0/br/deed.en

Authors' images on the cover and the half-title page: by courtesy of Aniket Mishra
Contents Page background: Gevorg Ghazaryan/Shutterstock.com
Word search puzzles: Created using the Word Search Generator on Super Teacher Worksheets (www.superteacherworksheets.com)
Crossword puzzles: Created using the Crossword Puzzle Generator on Super Teacher Worksheets (www.superteacherworksheets.com)
FIFA 2026 Poster: Fair Use/DatBot/https://en.wikipedia.org/wiki/File:WorldCup2026lposter.jpg
FIFA 2026 Schedule: by courtesy of Shubhali Chopra and Yukta Vats

1930 World Cup

From top, clockwise: The ball chosen by the Argentina team: CCA-SA 3.0 Unported/Soerfm/Oldelpaso/https://commons.wikimedia.org/wiki/File:1930_World_Cup_Final_ball_Argentina.jpg; The ball chosen by the Uruguay team: CCA-SA 3.0 Unported/ Soerfm/Oldelpaso/https://commons.wikimedia.org/wiki/File:1930_World_Cup_Final_Ball_Uruguay.jpg; Estadio Centenario: PD; Jules Rimet: PD/Bibliothèque nationale de France, Agence de presse Mondial Photo-Presse; Estadio Centenario Final match: PD/Centro de Fotografía de Montevideo

1934 World Cup

From top, clockwise: Ricardo Zamora and Gianpiero Combi: PD/Danyele; Federale 102: CCA-SA 3.0 Unported/MDBR/https://commons.wikimedia.org/wiki/File:Federale_102.jpg; Matthias Sindelar: PD/Caio Brandão Costa/Storie di Calcio; Italy's celebration: PD/Fma12; Coppa Del Duce: PD/Skblzz1/Le Miroir des sports, 12 juin 1934, p.392

1938 World Cup

From top, clockwise: Trophy presentation to Giuseppe Meazza: PD/Skblzz1/Excelsior, et Le Journal; Ernst Wilimowski: PD/Pit rock; Mo Heng Tan: CCA-SA 4.0 International/Abuhabibah91/ https://commons.wikimedia.org/wiki/File:Tan_Mo_Heng.jpg; World Cup final: PD/Skblzz1/Le Miroir des sports

1950 World Cup

Left page, from top, clockwise: Gre-No-Li: PD/Mr Bullitt-commonswiki/AFTONBLADETS ARKIV; Superga tragedy: PD/Danieletorino2/sconosciuto; Estadio Maracana: PD/Arquivo Nacional Collection/DarwIn; The Swedish team: Common Cultural Heritage PD/Carlos, I; A stranger; The Italian team: Common Cultural Heritage PD/ Carlos yo/Unknown author; Ghiggia with the trophy: Common Cultural Heritage PD/ Carlos yo/Unknown author; **Right page, from top to bottom**: Ghiggia's goal: PD/Fma12; Grande Torino: PD/Danieletorino2; Indian Olympic team: PD–India/ Drat8sub/The Hindu

1954 World Cup

From top, clockwise: Trophy presentation: PD/Carlos yo/Unknown author; World Cup captains: PD/Skblzz1/Liebig Milano - serie n°289 LEMCO; The Golden Generation: CCA-SA 3.0 Unported/ Hello world/Tibor Erky-Nagy/https://commons.wikimedia.org/wiki/File:Golden_Team_1953.jpg; World Cup final: CCA-SA 4.0 International/Regasterios/ETH-Bibliothek Zürich/

Unknown author – Comet Photo AG (Zürich)/https://commons.wikimedia.org/wiki/File:Fussball-Weltmeisterschaft_1954_(Com_M03-0108-005-0004).jpg

1958 World Cup

From top to bottom: Battle of Santiago: Common Cultural Heritage PD/B1mbo/; Brazilian Team: PD/999real/Associated Press/*El Gràfico*; **bottom left**: Pelé PD/Fma12/*El Gràfico*; **bottom right**: Brazilian team winning the Cup: PD/Bonkers

1962 World Cup

Left page, from top to bottom: Dittborn: CCA 4.0 International/Rec79/ Desconocido - Colección: Colección privada de la familia del Solar Donoso/ https://commons.wikimedia.org/wiki/File:5.H%C3%A9ctor-del-Solar-con-Dittborn-Pdte.-del-Comit%C3%A9-Chileno-del-Mundial-de-Football-en-Talca_(1).png; Estadio Carlos Dittborn: Common Cultural Heritage PD/ SuperSkaterDude45/Nežinoma; **Right page, from top to bottom**: Amarildo Tavares: PD/Danyele; Italian team: PD/Danyele

1966 World Cup

Left page, from top to bottom: Challenge 4-Star: CCA-SA 3.0 Unported/ MDBR/ https://commons.wikimedia.org/wiki/File:Challenge_4-star-1966.jpg; World Cup Willie: CCA-SA 4.0 International/Kingsif/Hmickey/ https://commons.wikimedia.org/wiki/File:National_Football_Museum_displays_7.jpg; **Right page, from top to bottom**: Blue plaque honouring Pickles: CCA-SA 4.0 International/ Mpilcher84/ https://commons.wikimedia.org/wiki/File:PicklesSignBeulahHill.jpg; The Champions statue: CCA 2.0 Generic/ Ham II/Matt Brown/ https://commons.wikimedia.org/wiki/File:World_Cup_sculpture_(cropped).jpg

1970 World Cup

From top to bottom: **top left**: Carlos Alberto's goal: PD/Enriquecardova at English Wikipedia; **top right**: Rivellino's Patada free-kick: PD/Enriquecardova at English Wikipedia; **bottom**: Pelé with Mário Zagallo: Public domain / Arquivo Nacional Collection/ https://commons.wikimedia.org/wiki/File:Zagalo_e_Pel%C3%A9,_Fundo_Correio_da_Manh%C3%A3.tif?page=1

1974 World Cup

From top, clockwise: Australia's debut: CCA-SA 3.0 Germany/Bundesarchiv, Bild 183-N0615-0012 / Mittelstädt, Rainer / CC-BY-SA 3.0/Sebastian Wallroth/https://commons.wikimedia.org/wiki/File:Bundesarchiv_

Bild_183-N0615-0012,_Fu%C3%9Fball-WM,_DDR_-_Australien_2-0.jpg; Yugoslavia at the World Cup: CCA-SA 3.0 Germany/Bundesarchiv, Bild 183-N0618-0045 / CC-BY-SA 3.0/Syrcro/https://commons.wikimedia.org/wiki/File:Bundesarchiv_Bild_183-N0618-0045,_Fu%C3%9Fball-WM,_Jugoslawien_-_Zaire_9-0.jpg; Johan Cruyff: CCA-SA 3.0 Germany/ Linksfuss/ Bundesarchiv_Bild_183-N0716-0314,_Fußball-WM,_BRD_-_Niederlande_2-1.jpg: Mittelstädt, Rainer/derivative work: Linksfuss (talk)/ https://commons.wikimedia.org/wiki/File:Bundesarchiv_Bild_183-N0716-0314,_Fu%C3%9Fball-WM,_BRD_-_Niederlande_2-1a.jpg; West Germany players with the Trophy: CC0 1.0 Universal Public Domain Dedication/Bert Verhoeff / Anefo/Alfvanbeem/Collectie / Archief: Fotocollectie Anefo; West Germany team photo: CC0 1.0 Universal Public Domain Dedication/Bert Verhoeff / Anefo/Alfvanbeem/Collectie / Archief: Fotocollectie Anefo; Sample ticket: PD/Ingridchen

1978 World Cup

From top to bottom: top left: Poster: CCA-SA 4.0 International/Pierre Grenet/ https://commons. wikimedia.org/wiki/File:Brecht_(2)_-_Copie.jpg; **top right**: Poster 2: CCA-SA 4.0 International/Pierre Grenet/Jean-Francois Batellier/ https://commons.wikimedia.org/wiki/File:Coba_affiche.jpg; **middle**: Opening ceremony: PD/Unknown Author/Crispybeatle/ https://commons.wikimedia.org/wiki/File:FIFA_World_Cup_1978_ceremony_at_the_River_Plate_Stadium.png; bottom: Tango Durlast: CCA-SA 4.0 International/ Gapac/https://commons.wikimedia.org/wiki/File:TANGO_MUNDIAL_78.jpg;

1982 World Cup

From top to bottom: **top left**: Tango España: CCA-SA 2.0 Generic/ Warren Rohner from Cape Town, South Africa/https://www.flickr.com/photos/50811886@N00/4593417700/ Tango Espaa]/ https://ta.wikipedia.org/wiki/%E0%AE%AA%E0%AE%9F%E0%AE%BF%E0%AE%AE%E0%AE%AE%E0%AF%8D:Adidas_Tango_Espa%C3%B1a.jpg; **top right**: Naranjito: fifg/Shutterstock.com; **bottom**: Paolo Rossi mural: JoaCaf/Shutterstock.com

1986 World Cup

Left page, from top to bottom: **top left**: Azteca: CCA 2.0 Generic/MDBR/ shine2010/https://commons.wikimedia.org/wiki/File:Adidas_Azteca_1986.jpg; **top right**: Pique: Fair Use/Georgethewriter/https://en.wikipedia.org/wiki/ File:1986_FIFA_World_Cup_official_Mascot.png; **bottom**: Maradona mural: Mark Green/Shutterstock.com; **Right page, from top to bottom**: **top left**:

Hand of God detailed: PD/Enriquecardova at English Wikipedia/Nick; **top right**: Jesper Olsen: CCO 1.0 Universal Public Domain Dedication/SVTCobra/ Marcel Antonisse / Anefo/ Collectie / Archief: Fotocollectie Anefo; **bottom, from left to right**: Stamp 1,2 and 3: spatuletail/Shutterstock.com

1990 World Cup

From top, clockwise: Etrusco Unico: CCA 2.0 Generic/TaurusEmerald/2010 World Cup - Shine 2010 from Johannesburg, South Africa/ https://commons.wikimedia.org/wiki/File:1990_-Etrusco_(Unico)_(4170713865).jpg; Fiat Panda Italia'90: CCA-SA 4.0 International/Carblogger/ https://commons.wikimedia.org/wiki/File:Fiat_Panda_Italia_90.jpg; Mars chocolates: CCA-SA 3.0 Unported/Mr.Nostalgic/Museum Rotterdam/ https://commons.wikimedia.org/wiki/File:Zwart_cilindrisch_blik_met_afbeelding_van_voetbal-doel_met_publiek_en_mascotte_van_%E2%80%9CItalia_%E2%80%9890%E2%80%9D,_op_deksel_wereldcup,_Mars,_objectnr_77271.JPG

1994 World Cup

From top, clockwise: Questra: CCA 2.0 Generic/Amakuru/2010 World Cup - Shine 2010 from Johannesburg, South Africa/https://commons.wikimedia.org/wiki/File:1994_-_Questra_(USA).jpg; Striker on a Coca-Cola can: Wachira W/Shutterstock.com; Bulgaria vs Germany: CCA-SA 4.0 International/Jonathan Schilling/ https://commons.wikimedia.org/wiki/File:World_Cup_1994_-_Bulgaria_v_Germany_-_stadium_board_with_final_score.jpg

1998 World Cup

From top, clockwise: Tartan Army: CCA-SA 3.0 Unported/The original uploader was Clio64 at French Wikipedia/GNU Free Documentation License/ https://commons.wikimedia.org/wiki/File:Fansecosse1998.jpg; Tricolore: CCA 2.0 Generic/Alza08/2010 World Cup - Shine 2010 from Johannesburg, South Africa/https://commons.wikimedia.org/wiki/File:1998_-_Tricolore_(France)_(4170715889).jpg; Footix: fifg/Shutterstock.com; Japan qualifies: CCA-SA 3.0 Unported/Hyolee2/ ja:User:Fk/GNU Free Documentation License/https://commons.wikimedia.org/wiki/File:19971116scoreboard.jpg

2002 World Cup

From top to bottom: Suwon World Cup stadium: CCA-SA 3.0 Unported/ Fetx2002/본인/ https://commons.wikimedia.org/wiki/File:20121003_Suwon_vs_Seoul.jpg; Fevernova: CCA-SA 4.0 International/Nicola/ https://commons.

wikimedia.org/wiki/File:Deutsches_Fu%C3%9 Fballmuseum_2015_2-Fevernova.jpg; Seoul Plaza: CC0 1.0 Universal Public Domain Dedication/ Phonet/ijs/ https://commons.wikimedia.org/wiki/File:Seoul_Plaza_2002_FIFA_World_Cup.jpg

2006 World Cup

Left page: Cheat sheet: PD/Frodar/Andreas Köpke; **Right page, from top to bottom**: French pennant: CCA-SA 4.0 International/Liondartois/ https://commons.wikimedia.org/wiki/File:Fanion_finale_de_la_Coupe_du_Monde_2006_(Italie_-_France),_mus%C3%A9e_national_du_sport_(Nice).JPG; Final game: CCA 2.0 Generic/Batman.94/David Ruddell/https://commons.wikimedia.org/wiki/File:Italy_vs_France_2006.jpg

2010 World Cup

From top to bottom: Vicente del Bosque with the World Cup: CCA-SA 2.0 Generic/Anthony Stanley/https://en.wikipedia.org/wiki/File:FIFA_World_Cup_2010_Spain_with_cup.jpg; Vuvuzelas: CCA 3.0 Brazil/BrokenSphere/ Marcello Casal Jr//ABr/https://en.wikiquote.org/wiki/File:Watching_South_Africa_%26_Mexico_match_at_World_Cup_2010-06-11_in_Soweto_7.jpg; Jabulani: CCA 2.0 Generic/Alza08/Shawn Smith from Astoria, NY, USA/ https://commons.wikimedia.org/wiki/File:Adidas_Jabulani_Official_World_Cup_2010_(4158450149).jpg

2014 World Cup

Right page, from top to bottom: Bastian Schweinsteiger: CCA 3.0 Brazil/Forgottenous/Marcello Casal Jr/Agência Brasil/ https://commons.wikimedia.org/wiki/File:Bastian_Schweinsteiger_celebrates_at_the_2014_FIFA_World_Cup_(cropped).jpg; **bottom left**: Brazuca: CCA-SA 4.0 International/Randy110912/Zakarie Faibis/https://commons.wikimedia.org/wiki/File:Brazuca.jpg; **bottom right**: Clovis Fernandes: CCA 3.0 Unported/VredanCovek/ Uploaded a work by Cyril Martino from https://www.youtube.com/watch?v=KS_WBLkfUSk&ab_channel=CyrilMartino with UploadWizard/ Cyril Martino/ YouTube: https://www.youtube.com/watch?v=KS_WBLkfUSk&ab_channel=CyrilMartino – View/save archived versions on archive.org/ https://commons.wikimedia.org/wiki/File:Clovis_Fernandes_2015.png; **Left page, from top to bottom**: Germany lifts the World Cup: CCA 3.0 Brazil/Stemoc/Marcello Casal Jr/Agência Brasil/ https://commons.wikimedia.org/wiki/File:Germany_lifts_the_2014_FIFA_World_Cup.jpg; Opening ceremony: CCA-SA 3.0 Unported/Legionarius/ Danilo Borges/Portal da Copa/ https://commons.wikimedia.org/

wiki/File:Arena_Corinthians_Opening.jpg; Messi in the finals: CCA 3.0 Brazil/FMSky/Agência Brasil/ https://commons.wikimedia.org/wiki/File:Germany_and_Argentina_face_off_in_the_final_of_the_World_Cup_2014_04_crop.jpg

2018 World Cup

From top to bottom: Mbappé winning the Silver ball: CCA 4.0 International/Kremlin.ru/PhilipTerryGraham /Russian Presidential Press and Information Office/https://commons.wikimedia.org/wiki/File:Kylian_Mbapp%C3%A9_receives_the_best_young_player_award_at_the_2018_Football_World_Cup_Russia.jpg; **middle left**: Telstar 18: CCA-SA 3.0 Unported/Ralf Roletschek / Дмитрий Садовников/ GNU Free Documentation License/https://commons.wikimedia.org/wiki/File:Adidas_Telstar_18_in_Russia_vs._Argentina.jpg; **middle right**: France with the Cup: CCA 4.0 International/Kremlin.ru/PhilipTerryGraham /Russian Presidential Press and Information Office/https://commons.wikimedia.org/wiki/File:France_champion_of_the_Football_World_Cup_Russia_2018.jpg; **bottom left**: Zabivaka: CCA-SA 3.0 Unported/Sergkarman/ Дмитрий Пукалик/ GNU Free Documentation License/https://commons.wikimedia.org/wiki/File:Rus-IvoryCoast_(13).jpg; **bottom right**: Fan ID: CCA 3.0 Unported/digital.gov.ru/Russian Rocky/*minsvyaz.ru.*/ https://commons.wikimedia.org/wiki/File:FIFA_World_Cup_2018_FAN_ID.jpg

2022 World Cup

Left page, from top, clockwise: Mbappé celebrates his goal: CCA 4.0 International/Tasnim News Agency/Lorenzo De Leonardis2 /حسین ظهروند/ https://commons.wikimedia.org/wiki/File:2022_FIFA_World_Cup_France_4%E2%80%931_Australia_-_(7)_(cropped).jpg; Argentina and Mexico: CCA 4.0 International/Tasnim News Agency/ AFC Vixen/ Hossein Zohrevand/ https://commons.wikimedia.org/wiki/File:Argentina_vs_mexico_2022_presentacion.jpg; Argentina fans at the Obelisco: CCA-SA 4.0 International/Adrielriv/Adriel Rivera/ https://commons.wikimedia.org/wiki/File:Fiesta_en_el_Obelisco.jpg; Al Rihla: CCA-SA 4.0 International/MS Sakib/HyperionLEO/https://commons.wikimedia.org/wiki/File:Al-Rihla_(cropped).jpg; FIFA president with host country leaders: CCA 4.0 International/Kremlin.ru/ Russian Presidential Press and Information Office/MasterRus21thCentury/https://commons.wikimedia.org/wiki/File:Rusia_entreg%C3%B3_el_relevo_de_la_antorcha_de_la_Copa_del_Mundo_a_Qatar.jpg; **Right page**: Messi with the World Cup: Fabideciria/Shutterstock.com.

The official poster for FIFA 2026

ROUND OF 32

28 JUNE

MATCH 73
LOS ANGELES
MATCH WINNER:

29 JUNE

MATCH 74
BOSTON
MATCH WINNER:

MATCH 75
MONTERREY
MATCH WINNER:

MATCH 76
HOUSTON
MATCH WINNER:

30 JUNE

MATCH 77
NEW YORK/NEW JERSEY
MATCH WINNER:

MATCH 78
DALLAS
MATCH WINNER:

MATCH 79
MEXICO CITY
MATCH WINNER:

FIFA 2026

ROUND OF 32

1 JULY

MATCH 80
ATLANTA
MATCH WINNER:

MATCH 81
SAN FRANCISCO BAY AREA
MATCH WINNER:

MATCH 82
SEATTLE
MATCH WINNER:

2 JULY

MATCH 83
TORONTO
MATCH WINNER:

MATCH 84
LOS ANGELES
MATCH WINNER:

MATCH 85
VANCOUVER
MATCH WINNER:

3 JULY

MATCH 86
MIAMI
MATCH WINNER:

MATCH 87
KANSAS CITY
MATCH WINNER:

MATCH 88
DALLAS
MATCH WINNER:

FIFA 2026

ROUND OF 16

4
JULY

MATCH 89
PHILADELPHIA
MATCH WINNER:

MATCH 90
HOUSTON
MATCH WINNER:

5
JULY

MATCH 91
NEW YORK/NEW JERSEY
MATCH WINNER:

MATCH 92
MEXICO CITY
MATCH WINNER:

6
JULY

MATCH 93
DALLAS
MATCH WINNER:

MATCH 94
SEATTLE
MATCH WINNER:

7
JULY

MATCH 95
ATLANTA
MATCH WINNER:

MATCH 96
VANCOUVER
MATCH WINNER:

FIFA 2026

QUARTER-FINALS

9 JULY

MATCH 97
BOSTON
MATCH WINNER:

10 JULY

MATCH 98
LOS ANGELES
MATCH WINNER:

11 JULY

MATCH 99
MIAMI
MATCH WINNER:

MATCH 100
KANSAS CITY
MATCH WINNER:

SEMI-FINALS

14 JULY

MATCH 101
DALLAS
MATCH WINNER:

15 JULY

MATCH 102
ATLANTA
MATCH WINNER:

FIFA 2026

FINAL

18
JULY

MATCH 103 (BRONZE FINAL)
MIAMI
MATCH WINNER:

19
JULY

MATCH 104
**NEW YORK/
NEW JERSEY**
MATCH WINNER:

FIFA 2026